Time Line Therapy®
Made Easy

Sidonia Press
Henderson, NV, 89012
USA

Sidonia Press and logo are registered trademarks of Adriana S. James

Library of Congress Control Number: 2016909599

James, Adriana Simona
    TIME LINE THERAPY® MADE EASY
    An Easy Method to Let Go of Negative Emotions and Limiting
    Decisions from Your Life
    192 p
    ISBN: 978-0-692-32883-5
    ISBN: 978-0-692-32884-2

Published in the United States by Sidonia Press

First Printing: 2013
Second Printing: 2016

Cover Concept and Illustration by Andrei Manescu
Back cover photo of author © Adriana S. James

Manufactured in the United States of America

Time Line Therapy® Made Easy

An Easy Method
to Let Go of Negative Emotions
and Limiting Decisions from Your Life

Second Revised Edition

Adriana S. James M.A., Ph.D.

Sidonia Press

Also by Adriana S. James

The Secret of Creating Your Future° (with Tad James)

Values and The Evolution of Consciousness
The Sources of Conflict in Our Modern Values

To the countless people
who search for a way of freeing themselves from
Negative Emotions and Limiting Decisions
and to their success for further progress in life

Contents

Acknowledgements

Writing this book has been an exciting but challenging undertaking. The work of simplifying Time Line Therapy® was not an easy one. The techniques of Time Line Therapy® are extremely powerful and there is always the possibility for a margin of error for a person who just begins the journey.

Although not designed to teach Time Line Therapy®, the purpose of this book is to introduce the public to the idea that life is more than the experience of negative states, limiting decisions, or limiting beliefs about the self, what is possible, and the world around.

I would like to thank my friends and co-workers with whom I share the same passion, for their insights revealed during our exchange of ideas throughout the years.

I am very fortunate to keep in touch with many Time Line Therapy® trainers who pointed out to me the challenges they encounter while teaching trainings and seminars. They are all professional colleagues and we have exchanged many inspiring and thought-provoking conversations. Many of the ideas reflected in this book are born as a result of those discussions. A special thank you to them.

Finally, my husband, Tad James who has never failed to encourage my research, and who was, and continues to be, my greatest critic but also my greatest supporter. No matter how many hardships one encounters in life, the love and support from the closest people are one of life's great blessings. More than anything else, I am in the very privileged position to discuss Time Line

Therapy® with its creator to understand all of the thinking that lead to its conception, the power, and profound effect of its techniques, and simultaneously, its simplicity. This provided me with an invaluable source on which, later on, I could base my own developments.

Beyond these people, there are three very special friends and colleagues who painstakingly edited and proofread this book. Foremost I would like to thank Natacha Thebeau, who looked over the manuscript several times. Her careful work and attention to details, her insights, commentary, and corrections made an extraordinary difference. I also owe special thanks to Sue Brereton and Brett Ellis, whose work made this a better book.

More than all, I would like to thank you, the beginners on the journey of discovering that you do not have to be prisoners of your negative emotions. It is essential to know that no matter what you experienced so far, you can overcome the past challenges. Therefore, it is my absolute joy to know that people are searching for something that hopefully will assist their progress into a future with more happiness and a better life.

Adriana James
Henderson, Nevada
February 2016

A Note about Trademarks

Time Line Therapy™ is a registered trademark owned by Tad James and licensed to the *Time Line Therapy*™ *Association*. It is used exclusively by members of the *Time Line Therapy*™ *Association*. The purpose of this trademark is to maintain the integrity of the techniques and to protect the public from misinformation or misapplication.

This is because we feel that people with the **commitment** to becoming skilled in working with *Time Line Therapy*™ applications will find the time and resources for the training, and acquire the needed skills in order to use the term legally.

A major benefit of this is becoming part of a large and growing community of people who will offer support if one chooses to become a truly excellent practitioner and coach, of course, if this is the path that one is tempted to take.

For group support, or if the reader wishes to connect with people who share the same interest in Time Line Therapy® and its very powerful techniques, the reader is welcome to join us at our international online community at www.NLPCoaching.com

Disclaimer

This is a book about Time Line Therapy® techniques. At the same time this is a book about the reader's own self and his/her ability to create change for success. It is about new ways of thinking about the things that block one's development and how to discover the barriers that prevent one's best performance in life. It is also about the thoughts and mind patterns that impede one's progress and natural development.

As an introductory guide, this book is based on a series of techniques grouped together under the name Time Line Therapy®. These techniques include a series of processes all based on a very powerful technology, but they provide no medical or psychological diagnosis, treatment, or advice. It is meant for informational purposes only. The material presented herein is not designed as a substitute for professional medical advice or professional clinical training. It is the responsibility of the reader to gain appropriate consultation for his or her health and fitness in order to use the techniques disclosed in this book for any reason or goal. It is also the reader's responsibility to receive the training or certification needed for the application of these ideas with another person.

This book is not to be construed as a training in Time Line Therapy®, so do not attempt to use its techniques with other people since there are caveats in doing so.

One more thing before we start. In this book all names have been changed to protect the confidentiality of the people sharing their powerful life transformations.

We are what we think.
All that we are arises with our thoughts.
With our thoughts, we make the world.

Saying attributed to Gautama Buddha

It takes a huge effort to free yourself from memory, but when you
succeed, you start to realize that you are capable of far more than
you imagined.

Unknown Author

Prologue

In one of our introductory trainings I met a brilliant, good-looking young man, in his mid-thirties, owner of a manufacturing company, and in the process of finishing his Ph.D. Looking at him from the outside, this man had everything someone could wish for: good looks, intelligence, education, prosperity, and glowing health.

What he said, however, surprised me very much: "*I would like to be someone who is happy and doesn't care what people think about me, someone who is confident, and doesn't change just to make people like me. I would be nice and caring of friends and family, successful in my career and delighted to be alive. I would be who everyone should be: themselves.*"

During the next segment, we made a little inquiry among the students, and many of them admitted that in their day-to-day interaction with other people, they were putting on a mask, playing the role they thought they must play according to the circumstances. Many reported the feeling that they could not be who they were in reality.

The examples kept pouring in: I want to be Bill Gates, Marilyn Monroe, John Lennon, Bill Clinton, Albert Einstein, John F. Kennedy, Leonardo Da Vinci, Plato, Bach, Martin Luther, Joan of Arc, Alexander the Great, Henry Ford, Audrey Hepburn, John Rockefeller...

Based on that experience I started thinking: how many people are in the same situation and are not even consciously aware? How many people stop and ask themselves one or more of the following questions: Do I spend a lot of time wishing my life were different? Or that my family was different? What about my job? Would life be better if my job was different? More secure? Better pay? If I think of my financial well-being, could it be different? Oh, and let's remember health. How is my health? How is it really? Can I hope for more than just not getting sick? Maybe my health should be better! And then, of course, let us remember the physical appearance. Do I secretly wish I was taller, thinner, younger, prettier, more attractive, stronger, fitter? Do I secretly wish my past took a different turn, less arduous and filled with negative events? That I was different?

Over the years of teaching trainings and seminars, and based on empirical evidence, this author has arrived at the conclusion that most people have these kinds of thoughts.

Why is that?

To begin with, chances are that a person does not actually want the life of his/her ideal person. Most people want to bring certain qualities these "ideals" seem to possess into their life like wealth, fame, success, love, freedom, compassion, bravery, etc. So ask yourself this question: What are those qualities that I want in my life?

This Author's Story

For me, an important transitional moment happened somewhere in the mid-nineties. I was doing what I thought I always wanted to do: be a concert virtuoso and play classical music as a leader of a major orchestra in Sydney, Australia. From about the age of three, I began working toward the career that was to bring me lots of success, international recognition, and lots of satisfaction. Or so I thought!

I had surrendered my childhood play and summer vacations, though not willingly at first, to practice and participate in competition after competition, year after year with great success.

I never had time to play with other children, because aside from training and practicing the violin, I was also an A student.

In the Australian spring of 1996, I went to visit a good friend of mine who worked at a Natural Healing Center. Her appointment was taking longer than usual and, as I waited, I met this other lady who was trained in Neuro-Linguistic Programming (NLP)[1] and Time Line Therapy® Techniques, although I had no knowledge of this at the time. We started talking and soon developed a very deep and meaningful conversation. In retrospect, I could say that that lady had the patience of a saint. For about an hour, she listened to me talk about how unhappy I was with everything I was doing (or **not doing**), with everything I was being, (or **not being**), and of course with everything I was having (or rather **not having**).

I do not remember the precise details of our conversation, but I surely remember being resignedly dissatisfied with my job, with the people and situations in my life – and with myself. I remember knowing exactly what I did **not** want any longer, and that was pretty much everything that went on in my life at the time. My career was no longer fulfilling. I did not like where I lived, the people I was working with, and overall I had had enough of the rigid boundaries that kept me doing the same thing, in the same way, every day, which brought me nothing but dissatisfaction and boredom.

After about one hour of complaining, she asked me one single pointed question: "*What would you like to do instead?*" and my mouth opened but no sound came out. I could not answer that question. Little did I know at the time, but the question "*What would you like to do instead?*" is a typical NLP question used as part of several techniques for changing behaviors. It dawned on

---

[1] NLP it is a collection of techniques and methods for producing personal excellence. NLP works very well with all the *Time Line Therapy*™ techniques and we encourage you to add NLP to your plans for learning and success.

me rather quickly that actually I did not know what I wanted. "More happiness," and a vague idea of a "better life" went through my mind. I wanted better people to deal with and more love and appreciation for my hard work and efforts. But I had no plan, no goals, and no direction of how I was going to achieve that "more happiness" and "better life". My past personal crises and life experiences had transformed me from an optimist into a pessimist, and a skeptic. To top that, my thinking and feelings were not helped by the onslaught of negative stories from the media. Regardless, from the outside, I appeared to be a very successful person, and for the untrained eye, it was hard to comprehend why I was complaining. In my attempt to explain to myself why I was "destined" to be unhappy and dissatisfied, I tried a lot of things: past life regressions, numerology, Myers-Briggs, shamanistic practices and even astrology. The number of empowering books I went through kept piling up on my shelf, and although they all had charming messages, in the long run, they seemed to be only platitudes. I practiced positive affirmations and tried energy work, and I took motivational trainings, but none of it produced long-term change.

Life would seem better for a couple of weeks afterward, but then the old problems would reappear all the same. Still though, I had no reasonable or logical reason for not being perfectly happy. I was an exceedingly good professional, a good leader with tenure and a well-paying job. Australia's famous Sydney Opera House was my beautiful working environment. My life was envied by many people. And yet, on a personal level, deep down, I felt unfulfilled and profoundly disappointed.

That very conversation with the NLP trained lady was a life-changing moment. The question I was asked made me realize, for the first time, that all I knew so far, the high level of education I had attained, the studies I did, the books I read, the trainings I took, were just not enough. They were not sufficient to override the many reasons I had for believing I was not a success.

Something was missing. While contemplating the answer that I could not give her, a sudden realization rushed through my mind: **I felt stuck because I believed that I was destined to be unhappy.** The message going through my head was loud and clear. I had good reasons why I believed I was not a success. My mind had chosen to be a professional victim.

The new understanding was disappointing and exhilarating at the same time. On the one hand, I had to admit that I had to take responsibility for my own unhappiness. This did not make me feel very good, because in many ways it was easier for me to blame the world and other people for my unhappiness than my own actions, attitudes, and behaviors. But on the other hand, it was also exhilarating! If my happiness (or unhappiness) was truly my own doing, it meant that I had the power to change it. So, there was something I could do. My beliefs and thinking were not cast in stone and I had the power to change it. During that conversation, I learned about scientific and practical ways of changing my beliefs so that I could choose how I react to life's experiences. That in itself was a turnaround. But I did not stop at that conversation. Now, it was time to do something about it. My decision was taken: I wanted to live life on the side where the glass was always half full. So, I started my training in Time Line Therapy® and with it, NLP.

If you are reading this book, it is likely that you have already researched different ways of improving your life, career, and your relationships, or maybe even yourself. Either you do not feel fulfilled, or something is not the way you want it to be – the way it **could** be. You do not feel like the perfect being you read about, or hear about. You are not perfectly happy, satisfied, successful, and cheerful. If this is you, what I would like you to consider is that it is never too late to be that person. You can do it now!

With friendship.
Adriana James

Introduction

✳ The heart has its reasons which reason knows nothing of.
Blaise Pascal, Philosopher [2]

*✳ Your intellect may be confused, but your emotions
will never lie to you.*
Roger Ebert, Film Critic [3]

A cross society, and deep-seated within the minds of women and men alike, negative emotions, limiting decisions, and limiting beliefs are everywhere and nowhere. Throughout time, people have noticed and responded to feelings. Having feelings makes us human, and yet, there is a tendency to deny that we have emotions, especially negative emotions, and to squash their existence as something unwanted and bothersome. Few people want to spend much time thinking about their negative emotions or limiting beliefs, let alone find the time to figure out

---

[2] Martie G. Haselton, , UCLA, & Timothy Ketelaar, Center for Behavior Evolution and Culture New Mexico State University, Department of Psychology, *Irrational Emotions or Emotional Wisdom?, The Evolutionary Psychology of Emotions and Behavior,* p.10. In press, J. Forgas (ed.), Hearts and minds: Affective influences on social cognition and behavior. (Frontiers of Social Psychology Series). New York: Psychology Press., 8/18/2005, http://www.sscnet.ucla.edu/comm/haselton/webdocs/HaseltonKetelaar.pdf
[3] Ibid

their source and learn how to let them go from past memories.

There is hardly a person on earth who, without conditioning, never felt any emotions. Granting that it is possible to dissociate completely from feeling anything, as in the case of medication for traumatic experiences, or as in behavioral conditioning, but in general, feeling emotions is a normal human phenomenon. And yet, most people try to ignore their negative emotions.

The intention behind the writing of this book was not to give the reader another inspirational work or to teach the full body of knowledge called Time Line Therapy®. There are already many beautiful inspirational volumes in circulation. The consideration behind its writing was to create a small but concise self-empowering guide. This author's wish is to bring to the reader's awareness the potential offered by the science and art of Time Line Therapy® techniques. If we could share in this book the beginning of the process, maybe the reader will feel inspired to use it to his or her benefit. The intention is to help one understand how to let go of past burdens and create happiness and success in life.

Although this book promotes an unpopular idea, it is the author's firm belief that everything one needs in order to make a change, is already within. Based on the thousands upon thousands of people who have used this powerful tool to let go of negative emotions from past experiences, we trust that the reader, too, can create a much richer and more satisfying life for him or herself.

Time Line Therapy® techniques help to eliminate past negative emotions connected with past experiences. Without even knowing, these old negative emotions or limiting beliefs are limiting one's life, in the present. If these negative emotions or limiting decisions were to disappear, one could create the future in a way that empowers that person. It sounds simple and promising, and it is.

Designed as an introductory guide, this book is far from being a complete training in Time Line Therapy® techniques. It is by no means a complete guide to the complete body of Time Line Therapy® processes. To truly master the entire collection of Time Line Therapy® techniques, one needs direct supervision with live training – and much more time than it takes to read this guide. Nevertheless, it is this author's belief, based on many years of experience and work with thousands of students, that anyone can still use the simple methods described herein to make positive changes in any area of life, including one's performance. Everyone can learn how to use Time Line Therapy®, without being a trained therapist, personal growth expert, or NLP practitioner. Therefore, the information in this book is easy to read and to apply immediately. Hopefully, this will provide sufficient inspiration for the reader to learn more about these powerful techniques that help create positive changes.

A Bit of Background

More than thirty years ago, Dr. Tad James, a certified NLP Master Trainer, made a discovery while waiting for a ride home after teaching a training session. It was a rainy day on Bishop Street, in the center of Honolulu, Hawai'i, and one of Dr. James' students was also waiting for a ride. This student had a lot of anger over a past event, and she could not stop talking about it. It was one of those events that happen unexpectedly in one's life, over which one seems to have no control. Dr. James, who was experimenting with time lines at the time, encouraged her to "float above the time line." The notion of "time lines" is not new; it had arguably been around since the time of Aristotle, and, throughout time, it had remained the subject of many different healing approaches.

The time line is one's internal time machine. To make sense of past events in relation to one's present, the unconscious mind organizes one's personal history in relation to time, one event after another. Everyone has a time line wherein there are unconsciously stored, and consecutively held, memories, emotions, beliefs, and decisions. It is because of this time line that one is able to know the difference between today, tomorrow, last week, next spring, and year after year. This is everyone's internal personal record.

Suppose for a minute that one was able to influence this time line, and was able to alter the memories contained therein in such a way that one could remove limiting beliefs and past negative emotions that burden and limit that person's life. Consequently, suppose also that one's life could then become happier, more balanced, and more successful. This is what Dr. James had in mind on that rainy day in Hawai'i. Being a compassionate man at heart, and noticing the possibilities behind this assessment, he began the experimentation and later developed Time Line Therapy®. With it quickly came the realization that this internal record is also one's vehicle for Creating Your Future®.

> "Float above the time line," said Dr. James to his distressed student, "and go back to the past to that event. Remain floating above the time line. Where is the anger?"
> "Right there in the time line," said the woman, pointing down in front of herself.
> "Float above the event, and tell me, where is the anger?"
> "Right beneath me—in the event, in the time line," she said.

"Now float further in the past, before the event, and tell me, where is the anger?"

She said, "It disappeared!"

"No, don't joke with me," he said. "Where is the anger?"

"It disappeared!" she said, again. "I can't believe it! It's gone!"

Once he realized the importance of this discovery and the nature of complex unconscious interactions, Dr. James understood immediately that biology-driven therapy models were not giving a complete and accurate understanding of physical, mental, and emotional wellbeing. Human thought patterns are influenced by much more than chemicals and electrical impulses; they are the result of time, space, a conscious association of meaning, and an unconscious storage of negative emotions, limiting decisions, and limiting beliefs.

There is a flurry of public health crises related to poor diet, lack of exercise, and smoking. But still, few people, medical professionals or otherwise, talk about the negative emotions contributing to chronic stress. Nonetheless, neuroscientists study the relationship between mind and body, the mind-body connection. There are now more and more published articles that relate the presence of stress and negative emotions as having a negative effect on our wellbeing. For our purposes, we need to recognize that cutting-edge neuroscience is now confirming what the physicist David Bohm postulated decades ago. A repetitive nature of thought could change brain chemistry. This is no small thing, as many people regularly fixate their minds on repetitive negative thought patterns.

The incessant repetition of negative thinking, doubled by the presence of negative emotions, literally changes one's brain chemistry. Having done so, the altered chemistry, in turn, perpetuates more negative thinking. This places one in a perpetually unhelpful loop. If the original starting point of that loop, i.e. the source of the negative emotions and thinking, is not addressed, even if using medication, one will find it difficult to overcome this circular pattern. Although there is a lot of effort put into assisting people who complain of a host of negative emotions, from a purely materialistic approach science is beginning to recognize that the mental, emotional, and physical aspects are more than connected; they seem to be differing parts of a larger whole, a whole we call a human being.

✝ The desire to be perpetually happy without ever experiencing negative emotions appears to have more to do with relinquishing responsibility for one's life. Here is how this works. It is easier to take a pill than to go through the messy and challenging attempt to solve one's critical relationship issues. It is easier to drown oneself in alcohol than recognize that one needs to change something about one's career, and so forth. It is easier to blame the world for one's unhappiness and resort to brainless entertainment than to work toward the fulfillment of one's dreams.

It should come as no surprise that negative emotions are an intrinsic part of our life. Without them, we would never know when something bad happens. When we are scared, we experience knee weakness, lumps in our throats or shaking throughout the body. When we are frustrated, we might experience a wave of heat and a heightened blood pressure. When we are embarrassed, we blush. Our emotions have an effect on our bodies. But what about long periods of inner dialogue of a negative nature, when we beat ourselves up or revisit over and over again an event that made us feel terrible? What about those times when incessantly we feel not good enough, or we are unhappy with the life we live?

✦ In times of stress, our bodies release two hormones, cortisol, and adrenaline. These two hormones have the purpose of mobilizing all of our physical resources to deal with the stressful situation. The blood vessels dilate so that more blood is available to the heart and lungs, the digestion slows down almost to nothing, the immune system's function is suppressed, and all of this for the purpose of having us ready for "fight or flight." This is an excellent system for a body's reaction to stress. That is to say, short duration stress. Typically, after a short period of stress, the body returns to normal functioning and all is well. However, if one lives for longer periods of time in continual stress, eventually one would experience (1) a depletion of vital hormones and an exhaustion of the endocrine system and (2) a state of hyper-excitation of brain cells and vital internal organs due to the continuous release of the stress hormones.

Dr. James had used other NLP techniques before to assist people with a variety of business problems, but he now understood the importance and the positive consequences of being able to let go of stress-related negative emotions. All NLP techniques are useful, but most of them do not take the issue of time into account as a significant component for long-term change. If one were to change a belief today, the modified belief will affect future events. But what about all of the events in the past? They still influence the present moment as well as the future.

Because of this discovery, Dr. James started "beta-testing" the technique. Once the results were to his satisfaction, conclusive and positive, the process further developed through stages of refinement. The raw, un-chiseled form would eventually become the many different techniques now known as Time Line Therapy®.

In essence, Time Line Therapy® Training and Techniques can be an important part of overcoming negative emotions and limiting decisions that create chronic stress, which in turn could lead to addictions, panic attacks, phobias, decreased performance, a lack of motivation, and many other problems. Obviously, all of those limit one's happiness, success, and accomplishments in life.

As soon as one experiences how good it feels to just not be bothered by something that has been bothersome for years, one will have what we call a "forehead smacking moment." This happens together with the realization that one had an obvious problem that could have been gone a long time ago. It is indeed a "forehead smacking moment" because one realizes, maybe for the first time, that the solution to one's problem was there all along, hiding in plain sight.

Getting Used To Miracles

Getting used to miracles may be the reader's biggest challenge when learning about Time Line Therapy®. It will feel like a miracle once all of the baggage from the past is released. Although not a miracle but how our normal state of being should be, many of us are so used to constantly living with past negative emotional baggage or in a constant state of stress, that we begin to think that this is normal. We are so used to constant stress, that some people interpret the lack of stress as "boredom", and often find it intolerable.

On the other hand, doing the same repetitive and mindless tasks day in and day out can also create stress. Often times, students complain of excruciating boredom while in university classrooms or amphitheaters. Some jobs actually lack opportunities for growth or development. Boredom can make one feel absolutely exhausted, tired, and weak. If that were not enough, when one tends to focus on what is unpleasant or even unhealthy, or what makes one worried, or nervous, this makes the situation even more intense, particularly if this happens for an extended period of time. Admittedly, many jobs have indeed become boring. Considering how many people use employment solely for the purpose of earning money, when in fact, they have no passion for the job, there is little wonder why boredom can become stressful. In addition, when one experiences a lack of growth and stagnation, positive change is tough to occur.

In conversations with many of our students, we discovered that this seems to be an endemic problem, especially amongst the younger generation, although it often happens for the more active people of all ages. How many people indeed have the self-drive or stamina to keep themselves active and stimulated? How many people try to educate, or occupy their minds with something positive, or entertain themselves when they get bored? How many people can actually say that their job is the same as their dream career? These are simple questions, and yet, their answers could be very telling.

And then there are those who hold two or three jobs, and who are indeed burdened by fears and anxieties about the present and the future. However, even these people could be benefitted by the excess energy that becomes available once the negative emotions are gone. Maybe they, like everybody else, could think better and find out-of-the-box solutions more easily with a clearer mind.

When feelings of non-accomplishment begin to weigh one down, automatically, one fails to be productive, and vice-versa. The word "productive" in this context does not refer only to work related issues. To be productive, one needs to be creative, and to be creative one has to be in a positive state of mind and in a positive emotional state. That extends to all other contexts of life.

Consider then, that a mind burdened by boredom, stress and non-productivity can lead to bad habits. It is worthy to note that in today's economic situation, where good jobs are harder to find, this has become a very common situation. After all, we all need to make a living, and it becomes difficult to break free when one is stuck in a position where stagnation and unproductivity rule the day. It is a real piece of good fortune to be in a career that one can truly and honestly enjoy.

While being bored at school or at work is not a new phenomenon, boredom with life, in general, could be extremely detrimental. A consistent boredom, placidity, and lack of drive doubled up with an adverse pattern of thoughts either because of something bad that happened in the past or an imagined fear of the future, is to say the world is miserable, and nothing good could possibly happen. But, often that is not the case; often the problem is not with the world "out there" but with the world "in here", and usually, people are looking in the wrong place to solve the problem.

However, many times even people with great careers experience negativity, and stress. Seen from the outside, they could appear as though they have it all. And yet, on the inside, there could be a caldron of negative emotions, limiting decisions, and plain ole negative thinking. The human condition is not directly proportional to the amount of money one has in the bank.

✳The Human Mind is Marvelous

The human mind is an incredible instrument with immense

potential. Consider that everyone lives inside their own mind. And depending on how that mind operates, how it has been trained and formed, and how burdened it is by negative emotions, limiting beliefs and limiting decisions, at some point, it may decide to have a "mind of its own" - pun intended.

It has become almost a cliché to hear conversations about the need to control one's mind so that it does not run amok. But how on earth could a person be in control of his/her own mind if (1) this person is not sure how it works and (2) if s/he dwells mostly on how unhappy one or one's life is.

One thing that is not immediately obvious to most people is that the mind is not a fixed "thing." The mind parallels emotions in that it is fluid, changing, and moving. It needs activity and positive goals to dwell upon. The mind works overtime to allow us to function in our inside and outside environments. In this process, it is continually creating thoughts made of pictures, sounds, feelings, smells and tastes. It also evaluates things, one's behaviors, one's looks, the events and situations one is involved in on a moment to moment basis. This is no small thing. The evaluation of our actions and behaviors acts almost as an observer. If these assessments are good and positive, then the experience we have of ourselves in all contexts of life is happier compared with having negative evaluations.

It is easy to go through life without thinking of any of this. We have other priorities, and even if the topic comes up, many people will dismiss it as non-important. However, there is nothing more important than one's mind and one's emotional state. **A person's attainment of success, happiness, and personal satisfaction, all depend on that person's mental and emotional states.** We have spoken to many students who believe that if only they had more money, life would automatically be better. In the course of developing their private businesses, many have achieved their goals in making more money. In fact, a big number of them have created real material abundance. However, to their surprise, they had to admit that no matter their material success, and even if life was better from that point of view, it was far from being stress-free. And it all boils down to their beliefs, decisions, and emotions.

Our Thoughts Are Not Preset

The nature of thoughts is that they are in constant motion. One's thoughts produce mind statements and descriptions – good end (positive thinking), wrong end (negative thinking). It is not obvious to many people that they have a choice. In fact, the general idea is that one does not have a choice. But we always do. This is a secret not known to many and hard to believe. To exercise that choice, first, one must to do a mind cleaning, to get up from under the weight of negative emotions, and limiting beliefs and decisions about oneself.

This author's challenge to the reader is to discover the power to create those miracles we only hear about from other people, and to exercise this choice. She challenges the reader to find how much more power there is inside the mind than is it even possible to imagine. This, of course, only if the reader considers it to be of importance. And after all, she challenges the reader to discover that one is actually not a prisoner of the past, family background, financial situation, or painful relationships. A person is not even a prisoner of his/hers own genetic inheritance. Like the engineer who understands the "magic" of technology, it will become plain and easy to understand the power and possibilities that come from one's own beliefs and decisions. What seems like magic will be well within one's grasp. The problem with miracles is that they ask us to stop taking our lives for granted by allowing issues and limitations to stop us from receiving them. Sometimes, miracles will happen to us without our asking for them. But, they are always more special when they are of our own making.

Will's Benefit From Time Line Therapy®

Will is a coaching client who was reaping the benefits of Time Line Therapy® at his job, but he was unhappy with his relationship. He had applied Time Line Therapy® to his fear of success and was finally setting personal records for sales at work. One evening, bristling with frustration at something his wife said, he realized that he was "content" with being totally stuck in a negative place—in one of the most important areas of his life, no less: his love life. This was Will's first "forehead-smacking" moment. He realized the problem was hiding in plain sight.

He needed to go back into his unconscious mind and uncover the hidden source, the root cause of his endless frustration. He then discovered that what his wife was doing reminded him of a relative who took care of him as a child. This relative represented many bad things to his mind because she was always expressing contrary opinions, paranoia, and racism.

Will consciously knew that his wife was nothing like this relative of his, but that she just had a habit of expressing herself in a similar manner that bugged him. Even so, he could not help but feel a mass of negative emotions every time they were in this situation. After using our rapid and long-lasting method to release

---

the negative emotions from his memories, he noticed that his wife actually appeared more beautiful and attractive to him. It was like he saw a new person in her that he had never noticed before, and he fully reconnected with his love for her.

The application of Time Line Therapy® did not create love for Will, but the absence of negative emotions in his connection to his wife opened him up to the love he had first felt for her. The love had never really gone away; it had been waiting all along to be rediscovered.

He realized that he had not shared his discomfort with his wife because his relative was the type of woman that no one could get through to in conversation. His wife was not that woman, though. Will felt so much love for his wife that nothing could have possibly stopped him from reinvesting in the relationship. He ultimately had an easy time opening their communication and guiding her to express herself in a way that he could relate to.

Will's wife benefited from this, too, because she had been hurting. She had sensed that he was holding back from her and that he was becoming more distant. In fact, she had been unconsciously engaging in the behavior that troubled him—without even realizing it was part of the problem. Her behavior was fueled by her fear of losing him, and by her desire to punch through the alienation and reconnect with him.

By all means, Will was one of those coaching clients of which every coach wishes s/he had more. As he devoted himself to learning how to use these methods on his own, he found many ways to explore the new possibilities.

Test Yourself

Read the following statements, and note how often each statement applies to you on a level of 0 to 3. Mark your answers in the space provided.

0 = Never   1 = Sometimes   2 = Often   3 = Always

_2_ I am not knowledgeable enough; this is why I am reluctant to change anything in my life.

_3_ I never had anyone to support me and help me climb the social ladder.

_3_ I am afraid of failing.

_2_ I don't believe I can succeed.

_2_ I don't believe in myself.

_2_ I've never been given a chance.

_3_ My life is far from perfect, but I can quickly pinpoint the shortcomings of others.

_3_ I have always procrastinated with doing things for myself, even things I've long dreamed of doing.

_3_ I am afraid of the unknown.

_3_ I wish I had more self-confidence.

_3_ I have low self-esteem.

_1_ I have a fear of rejection.

30

0 = Never   1 = Sometimes   2 = Often   3 = Always

_3_ I pretend to be self-assured, but inside I am very timid.

_1_ I get the feeling that other people have it in for me.

_0_ I am jealous of others, and that makes my life difficult.

_1_ I am afraid of a challenge. In fact, I hate it. It's just too hard.

_0_ I feel resentful and critical when looking at successful
people. Why not me?

_0_ I have done a lot of inner work and have applied the Law of
Attraction, yet I have not succeeded.

_3_ I never felt really good about myself.

_1_ I am not smart.

_0_ I feel resentful and critical when seeing successful people.

_3_ I don't know how to take the fear of the future and change
it into something fun or exciting.

_3_ My dreams were just that – dreams. Life is very different.

_3_ I get anxious when I step outside of my comfort zone.

_2_ I would if I could, but I can't, so I won't.

_3_ I can't trust myself to step out and do something for myself.

_2_ I don't feel like I am free to do what I want.

_3_ I have always felt inferior.

_2_ I guess, I am simply not good enough.

_3_ I don't think people take me seriously, even when I am
being serious.

_3_ I don't follow through with my bright ideas; I talk myself
out of them.

_2_ I made mistakes in my past, that led to deep hurt. Never
again.

_3_ In my career, when I hear "no," I take it personally.

_3_ I am not an angry person. People make me angry.

0 = Never   1 = Sometimes   2 = Often   3 = Always

_3_ I don't know how to become self-confident. I am trying, but I don't seem to get there. So I am playing a game of pretense.

_3_ I am afraid of looking foolish.

_2_ I worry a lot about the future.

_2_ I feel guilty, even when I don't do anything wrong.

_2_ I had a difficult childhood. I'll never overcome that.

_2_ I fear not being able to handle objections from my boss, spouse or parents.

_3_ I don't set goals for the future; what if they don't come true?

_1_ I wish I could live my life over again. Then, maybe things would be different.

_1_ I am afraid that I am losing face and I will look like a fool.

_2_ It takes too long to get results, so it's not even worth trying.

_2_ I don't make decisions because I'm fearful and anxious. What if I make the wrong decision?

_3_ The best in life is not for people like me. I come from the wrong side of the tracks.

_1_ I blow up at my spouse/kids and it's always their fault. They really make me angry.

_3_ I've had lots of emotional pain in my life.

_1_ I feel angry and rejected when others don't like me.

_3_ I believe other people don't really understand me.

_2_ I can't decide because I feel very conflicted about what I want. I know I should want something else, but I don't.

_3_ I have always felt inferior.

_3_ I can't discipline myself enough.

116

0 = Never   1 = Sometimes   2 = Often   3 = Always

_3_ I can't find real love in my life. In fact, I wonder if there is such a thing.

_2_ I'm good enough to make a means to an end, but I'm certainly not an unusually gifted person.

_2_ If I change things around in my life, what would people say about me? They won't understand.

_2_ I want to change some things but I just can't get started.

_3_ People criticize me for being aggressive, but, actually, I become defensive because I am hurt.

_3_ I am supportive of my family and even my co-workers, but I tend to put myself down.

_3_ I didn't have good luck in my life, at least not to the extent that others did.

_3_ I do not perform at my best, usually out of fear or avoidance.

_3_ I had a lot of hardships in my life and I feel worn out.

_3_ I can't afford the luxury to change anything right now.

_1_ I am too old for change. You can't teach an old dog new tricks.

_1_ I think people around me are just too dumb.

_1_ I will always be overweight; it's in my genes. Nobody can do anything about it. Why bother?

_3_ All I know is work; I wasn't born rich, you know?

_2_ You have to put up with things you don't like. That's life.

_2_ I never meet the "right" people.

_2_ I don't have the talent or skills that others have.

_2_ I don't have anybody to help me. I am all alone in this life.

_2_ I was born under the wrong stars.

0= Never   1 = Sometimes   2 = Often   3 = Always

_1_ I didn't get a good education where I grew up. There is nothing I can do about that now and that's how it is.

_1_ With young children, my life will be chaotic for a long while.

_2_ I've always struggled with money. People with money don't care about me anyway, so what's the point?

_3_ I'm afraid of heartbreak because I was betrayed in a previous relationship.

_2_ I will always be lonely, even if I am in a relationship, so there isn't much I can do about it.

_1_ I worry that I am not a good enough parent to my children.

_1_ I am afraid that others judge me; they may see the worst in me.

_2_ I don't get paid enough to do my best work.

_3_ I cannot meet the right person.

_3_ My boss and co-workers don't appreciate me.

_1_ My family does not appreciate or understand me.

_1_ I don't believe I can do anything new, not now.

_0_ I was born in the wrong part of the world.

_0_ I am afraid of beautiful women. They eat you alive.

_3_ I stay away from handsome men. They're only into chasing women. And they won't look at me, anyway.

_2_ I am just a simple man/woman. Do you think I can really do what I want?

_3_ I don't know how to build a business of my own.

_3_ I lack confidence in my ability to manage myself.

_3_ I am not sure what I really want.

0 = Never   1 = Sometimes   2 = Often   3 = Always

_3_ I can't get rich working for others, and I am scared to open my own business.

_1_ I do not have enough "juice" to keep things going.

_1_ I don't have any desire to invest in myself. This is the way I am, and nothing can be done about it.

_3_ My spouse is going through a hard time. I must be there for him/her, so I can't do anything for me.

_3_ I am not important.

_2_ I don't make excuses; I am waiting for inspiration to hit me and when it comes I'll do something big!

_3_ Life is a rollercoaster. Whatever will be, will be!

_1_ If it weren't for my family/the economy/my lack of skills/ lack of education/my gender/my children/etc., I could have been a success!

_2_ I am always worried about what other people will say about me if I do or don't do something.

_2_ I live a boring existence. I wish I'd had more success, fun, and enjoyment.

_2_ I cannot begin any change because it's too hard to sustain the motivation required.

_2_ I will get to it tomorrow. Today I have too many worries.

_1_ I don't want to even try to see myself for who I really am.

_1_ I am not sure of myself, but I manage to get by.

_2_ I will suffer consequences if I fail.

_2_ People get on my nerves.

_1_ I had bad luck, and that's why I am stuck.

_1_ I'm too busy to do anything I want to do for myself.

_2_ I'm just not the creative type.

0 = Never   1 = Sometimes   2 = Often   3 = Always

_2_ I should be happy and grateful for what I have. Why try for more?

_2_ I have too much on my plate.

_3_ I have to work hard at everything. I'd like to have it easy.

_2_ I have never tried to change my life, what would make me think I can do it now?

_1_ I like to watch movies with people living an interesting and exciting life. My life is so boring!

_2_ The conditions around me are too difficult.

_0_ If you want to make it big, it won't happen by working honestly.

_1_ I live in the wrong town/ city / suburb.

_3_ I am not attractive enough.

_2_ I'm afraid I'm just not capable enough to hope for more.

_247._ Total Points

Instructions to the Reader

Add together the total number of points from this questionnaire. The highest possible score is 360 points, which are the total when you answer "3" for "Always" to each statement in the questionnaire.

✓ If the final score is 241 – 360, it is likely that you feel "stuck," stubborn, and highly judgmental of others. The rules you have adopted and the negative emotions you experience are creating barriers to your success in life. By choosing to change beliefs that limit you, and by letting go of the negative emotions connected to those barriers, you will experience considerable change for the better. This high score means that you will need to invest a lot of time and commitment to yourself to create your success, but the greater the investment, the more significant the changes you will make in your life.

If your final score is 121 – 240, you are in the middle of the road. We consider this as "average." Although you are encountering serious limitations to your success and sense of well-being, it will be relatively easier for you to learn how to change those aspects than it will be for those who reached a higher score. The change will come easier.

If your final score is 0 – 120, it is likely that you are one of the people in this world who serve as an example of prosperity, success, health, and happiness. If you are not, then go back and re-take the test with more introspection and honesty.

About the Questionnaire

The statements and questions in the above questionnaire are all related to at least one of the following: limiting decisions, limiting beliefs, negative emotions and rules about oneself. Some of them also show a lack of knowledge which is the simplest thing to correct.

Limiting decisions are statements made about oneself which prevent the achievement of one's fulfillment, self-realization, and true happiness. Here are some questions that are useful to ask: "Did I make a limiting decision at some point in my life? Did I ever decide, maybe only unconsciously, that I was not good enough? Do I believe that I cannot do something? Do I believe that I could never have something I want?" It is a good idea to spend a few moments to consider these questions. Too many people deprive themselves of prosperity and other forms of success without even knowing that they are mindlessly standing in their own way – all because of these limiting decisions, which may not even be theirs, but rather adopted from others.

Continuing, the reader should consider the following: "Perhaps I decided something against my best judgment because I thought this was required from me, even if I did not feel it was right." This might have been a long time ago and, though things have changed since, the decision is still present in the unconscious mind. Because these decisions of the past limit us in "the now", we call them limiting decisions. As long as the unconscious mind holds onto these limiting decisions, one cannot observe possibilities and opportunities – even if they were to be presented plainly. Time Line Therapy® makes possible the removal of those decisions, even if they were created out of fear or other negative emotions.

Limiting beliefs are beliefs about oneself are directly detrimental to one's personal wellbeing, career performance, happiness in relationships, and they could even influence all other areas of life. Some of these beliefs may seem accurate if, say, they regard one's physical appearance because of course one can legitimately say, "I am not tall enough" if one's height is only five foot tall. But, aside from the obvious, limiting beliefs can prevent or substantially reduce the ability to be successful. If the belief "I am not tall enough" becomes a hindrance to one's success and achievement in life, then it is a limiting belief. It is not the fact of not being tall, but the belief that because of not being tall enough, one has negative consequences that create the problem. Hapiness is not height dependent. These limiting beliefs are simply related to limiting decisions, and Time Line Therapy® uses the same process to remove them both.

Negative emotions are emotional states of negativity, which include anger, frustration, sadness, fear, hurt, guilt, jealousy, resentment, plus a host of other emotions which are bothersome and unpleasant. A simple and rapid method in Time Line Therapy® allows one to erase these negative emotions, as well.

Personal rules act a lot like beliefs, in that they are based on limiting beliefs or limiting decisions made in the past. If one were to say "This is just how it is in the world, and there is really nothing I can do to change my life," it could be that it is the case of a rule based on a limiting belief. For some reason, rules seem much more robust and resistant to change than other thought patterns, yet we probably all know someone who has changed his or her rules, thus changing their life. Personal rules are changeable much like we change beliefs with Time Line Therapy®.

Lack of knowledge is the easiest barrier to deal with, as one only needs to gain more knowledge or more training. For example, if one holds the belief that it is impossible to make significant changes in life due to a lack of motivation, the real issue is that some information or skill is missing regarding how to change one's behaviors. Then, simple logic tells us that one needs to learn and acquire the information necessary. Admittedly, many behaviors are extremely hard to change consciously, because no matter how much one wants to change, one really just does not know how. Most often than not, trying to consciously change a behavior, ends up in frustration and disappointment. This is because behaviors are not produced consciously. They belong to the **automatic** and **unconscious** area of responses which we use to act and react to life in general.

Take nail biting, for example. People who bite their nails do not wish to do this behavior, and they say to themselves, "I will never do it again." only to repeat the behavior despite the conscious decision to not bite the nails. Nail biting is a minor example but think of gambling, drinking, smoking, or overeating. If people could easily change these behaviors consciously, the behaviors would be gone already. But, they are not. As we shall see, behaviors are easy to change when one involves both the conscious and the unconscious mind.

It is possible to get rid of unwanted behaviors. It is possible to install strategies and behaviors for success in life. It is also possible to learn how to model successful people, people with great relationships and fantastic prosperity – so that one can have the same results. Unfortunately, the process is not as simple as copying what they do. First, one needs to find out what exactly these people are doing inside of their heads, their belief system, their strategies for accomplishment, their personal values, as well as their decision making process. Subsequently, one needs to learn how to install the same thought patterns, values, attitudes, decisions and positive beliefs in oneself. It's a matter of learning how to do that, and it is much quicker to learn than one might think, as long as the belief that it is possible exists in one's mind.

Knowledge is power. Lack of knowledge is lack of power.

The Potential

The techniques in this guide have the potential to allow the reader to begin the process of transforming one's life and the lives of others, just as they have for hundreds of thousands of people around the world. Therefore, it is important to start a process of introspection before one can proceed with anything. The positive changes could manifest in one or all of the main areas of life including

- Career and Business
- Health and Fitness
- Family and Relationships
- Personal Growth and Development
- Spirituality

The reader may consider applying the information presented here in more than just his/her personal life, because s/he will always find new ways of using these tools. S/he may even choose to embrace it as a new career, or add it as a valuable part of his/her current career as a coach or business consultant. Our desire is to have more people share this information and assist others to get rid of life's obstacles. It only takes a few minutes of watching television news to realize that there is already too much unnecessary suffering going on in the world.

A Straight Opinion to the Reader

As we proceed further, we would like to take a moment to address the reader directly, with some personal observations based on experience and empirical evidence collected during many years of doing trainings, seminars, as well as personal coaching. It is important to remember that it is worth the effort to develop new ways of looking at your own mind. Maybe you, dear reader, have never spent any time considering your mind. If you are like most people, this observation of how your mind works may have never occurred to you. But if you want, just for argument's sake, do this once. You may be amazed at what you discover. If you choose to do that, the process has the potential to deepen your understanding of how your thinking influences your actions, performances, activities, and, therefore, your results in life. Now, that may sound farfetched, but it is true. There is a direct relationship between what you hold in your mind and what behaviors you produce. And your behaviors will either lead to success or a lack thereof.

There is no secret in the field of psychology that there is a correlation between emotions and choice. In other words, your choices are tightly intertwined with the quality of emotions you feel at the time. Similarly, your behaviors are also intertwined with your emotions. We only need to think of how much choice is available to a person throwing a fit. They say the wrong things, they produce weird behaviors, and in fact, they do not seem to have much control over themselves. During their fit, they cut themselves off from all other possible options regarding different behaviors. They are in "it", and nothing that anyone could say or do will change that behavior. Even still, when asked, the person "having a fit" often feels unable to stop themselves, even if afterwards, they become consciously aware that the behaviors are unpleasant.

Negative emotions such as anger and fear are natural responses when one experiences an attempt from others to interfere with one's goals, personal space, choice, personal values, beliefs, or boundaries. Therefore, it is not our aim to prevent the experience of emotions. In fact, the presence of negative emotions is what makes us realize something is amiss. However, it is desirable to have our emotions under control. Apparently, the way we have been trying to do that so far has produced less than stellar results.

It is this author's opinion that emotions are more than chemical balances or imbalances in the brain. This is just the materialist aspect, which although helpful, is incomplete. Chemical imbalances are indeed found in correlation to certain negative emotions. But the interesting situation occurs when, those chemical imbalances are attended to, and one can still experience negative emotions. Nevertheless, if the situation is reversed, and the circumstances creating the chemical imbalance are resolved, the chemical imbalance seems to disappear all by itself. That merely shows again the relationship between mind and body and how interlocked they actually are. It has been this author's personal experience, and the experience of thousands of participants in our trainings and seminars, that negative emotions can disappear completely once the internal "environment" is cleaned up. But the process must start "inside" rather than "outside", because it is almost impossible to change the world around you. However, you can change your reaction to it.

The chemical imbalances do not seem to be there either. Of course, since the author is not a medical doctor, we cannot say with certainty what the chemical balance or imbalance is. All we can say is that based on the empirical research and the feedback we receive - the set of symptomology seems to just disappear. And this is where Time Line Therapy® comes in very handy.

✝ We Are Conflicted

From early childhood, we are blasted with conflicting messages. We hear things like, "Get on with your life! Get in charge! Forget about the past! Control your emotions! Learn some emotional intelligence! Think with your head not with your feelings!" Yet, at the same time, we are also at the receiving end of the exact opposite. "Listen to your heart. Get in touch with your emotions. Let your feelings guide you. Go with your gut. Express yourself!" So, which is it? What are we supposed to do?

There is truth on both sides of this argument. Yes, it is a good thing to pay attention to our feelings and recognize our emotions, but how can one do that if all one experiences are negative emotions?

The rational and logical approach typical of the western thought tends to discard the importance of emotions as something fundamentally flawed, and, therefore, to be avoided or, at least, controlled at all costs. Nevertheless, there is wisdom in an emotional response. This author is not the first to disclose that emotions are sensible, intelligent, and not to be ignored.

On account of the fact that when we experience emotions, we go through that process **instantly** and **subjectively**, those feelings stand as a sign of an instinctively positive or negative response. If we were only capable of noticing that process during that infinitesimally small timeframe, we could then rationalize our responses later on, and by extension, our choices and decisions. Therefore, it is also true that making decisions should not rely on an emotional impulse alone. This is particularly important when we are about to decide whether to enter, or leave a relationship. Likewise, it is essential for managers, who are required to make significant decisions on a daily basis. Business, investments, or career decisions should rely mostly on rationality and logic. Emotions are not really welcome in the business world, since it is a world based on numbers and percentiles, and figures do not have emotions. However, whether we are happy to admit it or not, emotions are here to stay - they are part of our human reactions.

Often, people make decisions despite their feelings. We have all heard someone say, "I decided to go that way, even though I knew deep down that it wasn't a good decision." Nothing is worse than making decisions when one experiences conflicts between emotions and rational judgment.

In conclusion, when making choices and decisions, it is best to have a mind that is calm, and emotionally unbiased. This may sound just like another platitude, and maybe it is. What is not a platitude though, is how to get to that emotionally unbiased state, when every person has had their own share of negative or even frightening experiences in the past?

The Learnings

Depending on the strength of the distressing experience, negative emotions in lesser or greater amount will make a person pay attention to the cause. Consciously and unconsciously, they will log into the memories of that event the impressions created by this unpleasant, hurtful, distressing, or difficult set of circumstances. This is how it is possible to store negative emotions or even limiting decisions and limiting beliefs, aside from the facts themselves. Notwithstanding the importance of the facts, at the unconscious level, there is another purpose for all of this sophisticated storage.

The prevailing theory is that we need to remember important events in order to activate different behaviors. Yet here, Time Line Therapy®'s record proves the opposite to be true. We do not need to remember the events and we do not need to remember the content of the events. This may sound counterintuitive. What we all tend to do, is to persistently revisit memories of upsetting events. But what is not commonly known, is that **the only real purpose for repeatedly revisiting a past event in our minds is to get completion on that event, to make it rational and to gain meaning from it.** Without finding **personal** meaning, one cannot achieve completion. Another way of saying completion is finality or closure. And without completion or closure, unconsciously, one tends to replay in their mind the event as many times as necessary, in the search for finality. Once closure or completion is achieved, the negative emotions, limiting decisions or limiting beliefs about that memory disappear, and it "magically" ceases to bother us. It is done. It is indeed, over.

It is worth mentioning that this process does not refer to "understanding" the emotions. Neither does it relate in any way to knowing "why" the event happened or why one feels a certain way. The negative feelings entirely disappear, and the memory becomes emotionally flat. At that moment, we stop stressing or obsessing about it. However, as mentioned before, this is not possible as long as we still harbor the negative states, decisions, or beliefs associated with that memory. What is relevant to get are the learnings, but more about that in a moment.

The drawback happens when we are mentally dwelling on the content of an event without completing it successfully. Thenceforth, all we do every time we revisit the event is to re-experience the old negative emotions, limiting decisions and limiting beliefs. That does not serve the purpose of letting go of the negativity stored in those memories. In fact, it may even act in the opposite manner, strengthening those emotions.

For the completion of the event to take place, and the negative emotions, limiting decisions and limiting beliefs to disappear from our memories and consciousness, it is paramount to arrive at the point of resolution for that event. In this context, the word resolution refers to finding the meaning of the event. This may sound farfetched since many events are not of our own doing and we seem to just "fall in" without any choice. And yet, when one manages to find the meaning and the resolution on an event, the negative emotions, limiting decisions, and limiting beliefs just disappear. In Time Line Therapy® we call this process, naturally, **the learnings**.

Consequently, the only thing that really matters is this resolution of past events by retaining the learnings. What are the learnings? While they are different from person to person, in a nutshell, they reflect finding the **personal meaning** and **consciously and unconsciously attaining resolution** on that event. There is a very practical intention in doing this and it has to do with trying to minimize current and future similar negative and distressing experiences. The learnings, for example, could act as future strategies and behaviors, designed to avoid the repetition of old and un-useful blueprints.

To the degree that the sources for a negative experience differ from person to person, one can also expect to observe differences in the resolution process from person to person. There are different levels of response to any event and many possible emotional reactions. In other words, the same type of event could be a disaster for one person while eliciting no more than a yawn from another. Many people have experienced frustration and hopelessness in the face of seemingly impenetrable limitations, and yet, they then created an excellent record of accomplishment with personal fulfillment and satisfaction. What did they do that was different? What made them pick themselves up and continue with a happy and fulfilling life experience?

It is impossible for this author to account for what all of the people in the past have done to achieve completion on past events, but we can certainly vouch for the participants in our trainings as well as for our coaching clients. They all have managed to get the learnings from past events, and find their personal meaning. This process has assisted them in attaining closure on the past so that they could freely proceed into the future.

NOTE TO THE READER: IF THESE TECHNIQUES DO NOT DO THE SAME FOR YOU, PLEASE CONSIDER THIS: YOU MUST FIRST MAKE THE CONSCIOUS DECISION TO CREATE POSITIVE CHANGE IN YOUR LIFE. MOST PEOPLE WHO DO NOT SUCCEED HAVE ONE INTERESTING CHARACTERISTIC IN COMMON. THEY FOCUS ON THE REASONS AND THE EXCUSES OF WHY THEIR LIVES ARE THE WAY THEY ARE, RATHER THAN ON WHAT THEY CAN ACTUALLY DO TO MAKE A POSITIVE CHANGE. THEREFORE, STEP NUMBER ONE IS TO ASK YOURSELF THE QUESTION, "AM I DONE WITH THE PAST? DO I REALLY WANT TO BE COMPLETE WITH ALL THAT HAPPENED?" IF YOU DO, KEEP READING.

yes and yes.

What Is a Negative Emotion

It is not immediately apparent that our definition of positive or negative emotions is of our own judgment. What is positive to one person may not be to another. The mind is an incredibly powerful tool, and based on one's rules for life, one defines what something is or should be. Based on this judgment, one begins to have different results. Therefore, one's very perception of an experience or situation has the ultimate power to dictate how one will feel, and how the mind and the body will be affected by that experience.

If someone wishes for good health, one must first ask oneself if he is ready to do away with the reasons for his illness. Only then is it possible to help him.

✦ This saying attributed to Hippocrates is very telling. We should also remember that Hippocrates lived about 2400 years ago. It stands to reason then, that this way of thinking is not new, but for various reasons which are beyond the scope of this book, they still have not penetrated our universal consciousness.

To complete this discussion, we can say that Time Line Therapy® is useful only if one is sure that s/he wants to change something in their internal environment. If that is the case, then this work will have positive effects not only on their emotional states in general, which will be more balanced and overall happier, but also in their interactions with other people. Just by being a different, happier, and more energetic person, one's relationships, at work, family or with friends, will be improved. Everyone loves to be around active and positive people. We all love to see other fellow human beings get over hurdles and attain success. We respect and admire that. Depending on what one manages to overcome, one could even become a positive role model for many of those people.

It goes without saying that a truly happy, successful, and fulfilled life includes much more than just going to the gym or going out with friends. If that were enough, we would already have a euphoric society, but regrettably, this does not appear to be the case. Another essential thing worth mentioning, although it is one of the elements least talked about, is the importance of a deep connection within the self. That is, being aware of one's interconnectivity between mind and body, which is just another way of describing the conscious mind and the unconscious mind. This is real freedom, self-reliance, and knowing inside that one is indeed good enough, without having to rely on one's outer world.

Knowing yourself is the beginning of all wisdom.[1]

[1] Attributed to Aristotle

Why Fear Paralyzes You

We appear to be fascinated with getting scared out of our skulls day in and day out. As a society, we face daily scary news and alerts, and we watch scary movies. Hearing or watching disasters has become almost a twisted form of entertainment. Some people even feel an appealing attraction to anything that is frightening. Can one get addicted to fear? Unfortunately, this is more of a common occurrence than not. People go to see scary movies to get scared while in a safe environment. Maybe this is to energize a very bland and dull existence, but they go to experience "the rush." At the end, usually, the movies result in some sort of solution. So the fear is experienced for a short amount of time, it creates a rush in the body, and then at the end, there is a solution. A boring life is worse than a scary movie.

There are a lot of scary things of which one could be afraid. Examples could include, lack of money, taxes, loneliness, feeling not being good enough, smart enough, slim enough, young enough. Add to that the fear of not being able to pay the mortgage anxiety regarding the children's future, fear of retirement if one is older, and unemployment if one is younger. Many people are fearful of not being liked, of being hacked on the internet, of terrorism, and of many other possible terrifying situations, that they envision for the future. People are panicking about taking action, and conversely, also that something bad could happen if they do nothing. They are anxious about changing things, terrified to say "no," afraid of being alone, worried about illness, afraid of loss, and the list could go on. There are so many ways in which fear keeps us stuck, that we could fill the rest of this book mentioning them all and we would probably leave out a couple of hundred.

Often, people are not even consciously aware of what scares them, but unconsciously, they respond to all fears. Many of these fears could even be irrational, which simply means that they operate without conscious or rational thought. If one really were to pay attention, one would realize that fear has a controlling mechanism in it. When one makes decisions based on avoiding things that are scary, or avoids making any decisions at all because of fear, one is not in control of one's life. Fear is. More about that will be discussed shortly.

If that were not enough, the outside world through the input of its daily news, confirms that there are a lot of things about which we should be afraid.

Commendably though, fear has many uses. First, it acts as a warning to keep one from entering into a situation that might be hurtful. It can also be used as a motivator to get away from something, such as a harmful relationship or a dangerous situation.

It has become habitual to hear one of the following pieces of advice: "Conquer your fear." "Feel the fear and get on with life." "Get to know your fear." "Battle your fears." "Address your fear." "Confront your fear." "Avoiding fear is wrong." However, what we do not hear too often, and what we are not taught, is how to let go of fear so we can really move on and be free.

Consider the following. Let us say that in the past one was involved in a situation that was extremely frightening. As a result, that person learned to be afraid. What if this situation were to happen again? Justifiably so, that person is now on alert. But being on alert, and paying attention to the outside environment in ways which are different from the past, is not the same as living in fear. Awareness is **not** fear. We would like to make something very clear. In this context, we are talking only about the fear accumulated in your body **from the past. Time Line Therapy®** **does not take away one's ability to feel any appropriate** **emotion in the present or in the future.**

It is not a well-known fact that **past fears residing in one's** **memories accumulate in the body and create reactions to life** **situations.** But they do. However, we are not the same people we used to be at that time. We have grown, and we have accumulated new skills to deal with life conditions. Hopefully, we have also become wiser. We have learned new strategies. We have matured. We have gained experience. However, the old fears are still inside of our old memories. Therefore, it is far more productive, and far better for our own development, to let them go so that we can move on and further develop or try new things, in a safe way.

Nevertheless, some people do realize that fear is not only not helping them, but that it is actually paralyzing. When one feels fear, one is stuck, like a deer in the headlights at night. Frozen. It is impossible to think clearly, when in a state of fear. Hormonally, the changes affecting the physical body do not allow for clear thinking or sound decision-making processes. This is what makes the difference between successful people and the rest. Those who have managed to "uproot" their fear, have found success.

Aside from being paralyzing, fear has the ability to create weakness, righteousness, and judgmentalism, and overall an inner world that leads to a failure-based attitude. This concept could be most difficult to grasp, but fear actually does not reside in the magazine article, in the newspaper, on the internet, or in the social media network, or anywhere else in the outside world. It lives inside our heads. It is in our minds and in our bodies. **Vulnerability, threat, and even danger exist in reality. But fear, as an emotion, is not the same thing as danger. It is a reaction based on a real or even perceived threat.**

When we were all cave dwellers, threats and dangers were used mostly physical. However, in our modern times, we face economic threats, financial threats, and many other threats that do not affect us on a physical level. Yet, if we allow fear to perpetually take residence inside our minds, we cut ourselves off from most of the opportunities that could help us to overcome exactly those situations of which we are afraid.

Fear as a Control Factor

But there is another angle to this fear business, and that is the use of fear to control people. As we have seen, physiological changes are happening inside the brain and body when fear is experienced. There is a part of the brain, in fact, the oldest part of the brain in evolutionary terms which controls the body's vital functions such as heart rate, breathing, body temperature, and balance. It includes the brainstem and the cerebellum. It is commonly known as the reptilian brain. This part of the brain has one main purpose – to assure the survival of the organism. When all other areas of the brain are asleep (i.e. during the night), this part is awake, because it is always fulfilling its primary purpose - our physical survival.

When one experiences a threat, real or imagined, this part of the brain responds automatically. To its most extreme, it really shuts off the rest of the brain. That automatic survival-geared mechanism is called the "flight or fight" response. This is a supportive response, naturally designed to help one escape danger. But most people are not well-informed; they do not understand that the flight or fight response is not fear at all. Fear is a secondary emotion which appears after the flight response fulfilled its purpose. If one does not fight, one flees from danger. The flight response could take two forms: (1) One flees to safety before the fear as an emotion is even felt or (2) one instantly freezes, and then fear sets in amplifying the freeze response. During the second possibility, one is literally stuck. The stuck state can last from seconds, to years.

Another important detail to remember is that in the flight, fight or freeze mode the entire body goes through a massive stress. At that moment, instantly, the blood is redirected to the essential organs of the body (heart, lungs, muscles, and the reptilian part of the brain). The neocortex (the big part of the brain) is left with only enough blood supply to keep it on, healthy but not in active use. During that time, one has little or no ability for rational thinking. Decisions and choices are made automatically by the reptilian brain for the purpose of in-the-moment survival, but without considering any of the circumstances that may follow. Literally, the activity in one's rational brain is suspended.

Therefore, if one's state of mind involves an emotional state of fear for longer periods of time, the body ends up depleted of vital hormonal and other resources. It requires a lot of work to deal with an immediate threat. The body works overtime, therefore, in time, one can end up with health complications. The immune system does not work as well as it could because it has become depleted. And then, without realizing it consciously, high blood pressure, high cholesterol, adrenal burnout, muscle fatigue, or depression, could set in, slowly but surely, often making one wonder where these issues are even coming from? It is much healthier and much more productive to let go past fears stored in the body, and to get out of perpetual tension.

Does Fear Control You?

It is not a well-known fact that, at the unconscious level, we record even the fears experienced during a movie. The unconscious mind responds to the suggestions from the movie, and then from that point on, for the rest of one's life, it will remember the fears that were felt during that movie.

Where did the zombie myth start? Why are we talking about zombies in our society as if it is something natural? And who are the zombies? Since when would one like to be referred to as a zombie? The consequences of adhering to this type of thinking escape most people. One wise question to ask could be, "What control and power does fear have over me, and how much of it is outside of my conscious awareness?"

If one lives in a continuous state of fear, many other possible inner resources are cut off. These internal resources are, oddly enough, the opposite of fear. In a state of fear, creativity and imagination are stifled. They cannot find expression. **Creativity and imagination are two natural human capabilities which, paradoxically, are necessary if one were to think "outside of the box" and find solutions** where somebody ridden by fear would be stuck.

There is even more to the fear factor. While living in fear, life experiences may feel somewhat "safe," however, in time this creates a culture of mediocrity and stagnation. If one does not take any action to do anything, one seems to preserve the "safe" status quo. Yet, this leads to no change. No change leads to stagnation and mediocrity. One cannot stay stagnant and simultaneously develop something new. A state of mind based on a desire for excellence and creativity will always find positive solutions to all the drawbacks and difficulties encountered in life.

If we actually care about being in control of our lives, we have to consciously decide that it is time to let go of unfounded fear, especially of those fears residing in the past. Not "to control" our fear, not "to get to know our fear", not "to face our fear", but to let it go. We need to consciously recognize that our life is worth living to the fullest and that we cannot do that if we live in fear. Aside from that, we also need to recognize that if we do not control our life, somebody else or something else will do it for us, through fear.

Once fear is gone from both the body and the mind, we can then proceed to do something which, in the past, could have been outside of our competence, and now it is not. Then and only then can we begin to take back control of our lives.

While in similar situations, some of our students have asked the question, "How is it possible that I was so stuck and I did not even realize? I thought it was just how I am." What they did not realize consciously, of course, was that scary movies, fear filled news casts, and their continued focus on what could go wrong had led their unconscious minds to this fear based "paralysis". Fortunately, when they got the learnings, they were able to let go of the fears and actualize a better life for themselves. Eliminating fear that was stored in their body freed them from their "stuckness", which allowed them to open up their future to more opportunities.

One Thought about Anxiety

Every person can relate to the following scenario since it is extremely common. At some point, we thought that some terrible things would happen in the future only to find out that those things never happened. We were anxious, only to realize that our anxieties were not founded on anything real. Meanwhile, we missed opportunities, did not try out possible relationships, did not attempt to negotiate the pay raise, did not dare to open a small business and to become an independent owner, and everything being taken into account, we did not act to any extent because we were afraid. We did not go for what we wanted. We did not make the decision that we could have made. We gave up. At that moment, fear controlled us, even if it was only in our heads. Therefore, as a solution, we could try something new. We could let go of past fears.

An important thing to remember is that Time Line Therapy® techniques will not take away one's ability to feel fear in the future. As a Time Line Therapy® trainer, and as a regular user of the techniques, if a lion were in her immediate surroundings, this author would run as fast as she could to safety. She would probably do that without trying to rationalize what she was doing. She would not sit calmly to analyze that she does not have any fear. As all other emotions, fear is a normal and natural reaction to an outside threat. However, it is not sensible to dwell on that fear for months and even years after the event, although it happens for some people. In fact, the ability to react safely could be enhanced if one were to release old fears from the past. Every small victory in the future will reinforce all that keeps us safe – and that is not fear. It is empowerment.

Fear as a Method of Conditioning

There is a school of thought that states that human free will does not exist, that any human action is simply the result of the consequences following a previous action. One takes an action, does something, and the result is either good or bad. This school of thought emphasizes the reward or punishment system in order to change behavior.[1]

This change is not necessarily for the benefit of the individual, but is dictated by the needs of the society at that time. Every generation has suffered from different reward and punishment systems, based on the needs of that era, as well as what was considered suitable behavior for that time period. What was acceptable during our parent's generation could be frowned upon now or vice versa, and this could be different again in the future. What we are conditioned to, right now, may very well become unacceptable to the next generation. This is where fear comes in as a handy tool – conditioning through fear works very well, unfortunately, just not for the individual. Then it follows that we could ask, how does fear condition us today?

Looking back at ones' past, we can all relate to having received a punishment when we did something wrong. It is easy to remember examples of this process from childhood. When we were in school, we got a pat on the shoulder and a verbal praise when we replicated the behavior we were supposed to reproduce, or, we received some form of punishment when we did anything different than what was asked. However, this did not happen only when we were young. This process is alive and well currently in our colleges and other educational establishments, with the difference that

---

[1] The author refers to Skinnerian operant conditioning.

corporeal punishment has been changed to mental and emotional punishment. Being laughed at, or branded with a demeaning or socially unacceptable label, could lead to embarrassment and shame. It could also lead to frustration, guilt, or other negative feelings. As this does not feel right, one can become conditioned to keep silent, hoping that in this way they will again gain acceptance in the group. Punishment and reward; break the status quo and one may be branded, keep the status quo and one will likely be accepted.

Even if most of our conditioning happens early in life, we can still create new fear reactions later on. For the purpose of understanding how someone can become conditioned by fear, let us look at an example from the level of an individual. In this scenario, a person, texting while driving, goes through a red light and gets a ticket. Because of that moment, that person, further distracted in thought, gets into an argument with somebody.

Now, we could exacerbate this even further. As a result of that chain of events, genuinely annoyed and grumbling, the person then tries to text their partner, only to mix up the phone number and ends up in a screaming match with his/her boss. Now, that person's job could be jeopardized. Still feeling the emotions of the day, s/he consequently ends up having a huge disagreement with their partner and, thus, their relationship could break, ending in a painful separation. All of this because of a red light s/he was too distracted to see and a focus on what could go wrong afterwards.

The perceptive reader has surely noticed already that the possibilities described above denote a predominantly negative focus when considering future possibilities, focus which is also derived from fear.

Subsequently, from there on, that person could end up terrified of driving through a red light. Does that mean that they will never drive through a red light, again? Unfortunately, it does not. However, they could constantly live in fear of driving through a red light, nonetheless.

Evidently, this is a fabricated set of connected events pushed to the extreme, and does not happen usually. However, it serves us well to argue the point and notice how easy it is to become conditioned by fear. It also helps us to recognize that fear from the past does not keep us safe. Rather, creating new strategies to pay attention to the environment and notice when the light turns yellow, combined with the good advice not to text while driving, would be far more efficient than holding onto a potentially paralyzing emotion while focusing on posible disasters.

This is how it works. One does something that results in punishment, and one learns to be wary of similar situations. If that type of situation happens several times (reinforcement), one then becomes conditioned to be afraid of comparable circumstances. It does not mean it will happen ever again, but it also does not mean one will never do it again.

Even the fear of punishment does not keep some people from repeating old patterns of behavior. As in our example, many people occasionally drive through a light that has just turned from yellow to red, even if they were ticketed for doing so in the past. Some people even lose their licenses temporarily.

The point is that the future has not happened yet, and still we are conditioned to be afraid of many things because of past experiences. **Yet, fear does not, and will not keep us safe.** Awareness, skills, and new strategies have a much better chance of keeping us safe in the long run.

NOTE TO THE READER: BEHAVIORAL CONDITIONING IS DIFFERENT FROM CLASSICAL CONDITIONING (PAVLOV), WHICH DEALS WITH AUTOMATIC OR REFLEXIVE BEHAVIORS.

Unfortunately, if we were to pay attention, we would observe that almost everybody is afraid of something. On a larger scale, even some big billboards are disgracefully trying to condition the population in a certain way. "Don't drive when tired, we're watching you!" Now, we are against driving when tired, however, cannot help but compare this sign with a set of signs on a New Zealand highway: "Take a break! Look at the scenery! Life is beautiful." Or "Stop. Revive. Enjoy the ride."

Anna's Story and Resolve Using Time Line Therapy®

We met Anna in one of our short weekend seminars called The Secret of Creating Your Future®. She was a good looking young woman, very friendly and talkative. During the first afternoon of the training, she had already made herself liked by everybody else in the group. Looking at her, she seemed to have it all together. Good looks, apparent intelligence, happiness, contentment, all seemed to be hers. She exuded such satisfaction in her life, that it was almost as if one could guess that her life had been worry free, sheltered with loving parents, great relationships, fun jobs, she seemed like one of the lucky people on earth.

It was not until the next day that we found out her story. We were talking about Time Line Therapy® and it's potential, when she stood up and shared with the group of participants her actual story. Severely abused as a child, she went down the path of drugs and alcohol. Realizing what was happening, she searched for help and managed to shed the bad habits. For almost a year, she was clean and her health and wellbeing started to return. Then, she met what she described at the time as "the love of her life". A very empowering and healthy relationship, almost like an unexpected gift after a period of hardship and a time of chaos.

But as often happens, the "love of her life" turned out to be a fiasco, and one day, her relationship disappeared together with the money in her account, leaving her in a world of debt and with the creditors at her door. At this point, Anna broke down. Desperate and alone, all she could do was cry and isolate herself from the world. There seemed to be no good options. The debts had to be paid, her ex was gone, and she was heartbroken and in despair. Moreover, she was paralyzed by fear. She could not act, and yet, she knew that she had to do something. Stopping for a coffee at McDonalds (by her own account, a treat she could barely afford), she sat down next to another woman who had had several Time Line Therapy® sessions with a trained coach. The woman recommended to Anna that she should try it out. She suggested that, if nothing else, it would help Anna her feel better, and release all her negative emotions, so that she could think clearly about what to do next. Baffled and confounded, Anna asked for the name of that coach. In her mind, there was nothing to lose.

The rest is history. Once the negative emotions from her past were released, Anna discovered that she had a lot of limiting decisions and limiting beliefs, as well as a very low self-esteem and self-confidence. After letting all of those go, her state changed dramatically. She described herself as becoming strong, healthy, and with a "newfound willpower". She did not want to let herself be defeated anymore by her life experiences so far".

When we met her in the seminar, she had paid off all the debts, got new qualifications and education, had brand new friends, and a job she loved. She acknowledged that her new friends did not know anything about her past. In fact, one of them blamed her for having a "too easy life" and that "she could not possibly understand" when she did not join in the blame-game of another friend. Once more, Time Line Therapy® proved to be helpful. The most interesting thing was that, as a result of the learnings she grasped, Anna's attitude, in general, changed. She was no longer the victim of her past and no longer a prisoner of her own negative emotions. Instead, she decided that despite her past life experiences, she would create an extraordinary life for herself. She became a licensed counselor working with vulnerable children.

Goodbye Guilt, Hello Future

Guilt and shame are two of the most destructive emotions. In spite of what we were led to believe, they have no value for us. As we shall see, the value of instilling guilt lies somewhere else, but it is not beneficial, despite the belief that it is useful.

Here is a question one must ask oneself to recognize the usefulness of guilt. "Do I know at least one person who feels guilt and yet does all sorts of unacceptable things?" If one is honest, naturally the answer must be yes. And this is the point. Guilt, as an emotion, has never prevented anybody from repeatedly making the same mistakes. In reality, the only things that count in these circumstances are individual values, guidelines, or rules for action.

Personal values are the motivators behind our actions, and that means that if one's own values are in line with the "Do no harm." principle, there is no need for guilt. Conscientious living and alignment with higher values are necessary, and ultimately, the determinants of our actions. Guilt and shame are a just a waste of mental power. **They really do not help us change our behaviors – they only make us feel sorry for the past.** Yet, feeling sorry for the past, does not mean we will never make mistakes, hurt others, or act out of integrity somewhere in the future. Therefore, we are submitting that by eliminating guilt, and incorporating resourceful learnings, new strategies, new values, and new behaviors and attitudes, one can ensure that old "unforgivable" deeds will never be repeated.

Guilt is not the same as having a conscience.

One can feel guilty and still repeat old behaviors or act

inappropriately toward loved ones. On the other hand, the learnings received during a Time Line Therapy® session on guilt, can install in the unconscious mind a different reaction to future outside events. Simply put, one can still have a conscience without allowing guilt to take over the mind and body.

As all negative emotions, guilt and shame have an unhealthy effect. Inappropriate guilt, held in the memories of the body and mind, can also unconsciously create repressed anger, or resentment towards those who (1) notice one's guilt and (2) use it to manipulate one's behaviors. After that, and as a result of (1) and (2), shame can also make things worse. This happens especially when one is not consciously aware of what is occurring in the environment, or when one does not realize what is happening until it is too late.

The guilt exercise described in this book, will not take away the ability to discern right from wrong, but it will surely lighten one's load of personal emotional "baggage." Our conscience can drive us to do great things, but guilt will only hold us back. In particular situations, we could become stuck because of old guilt.

NOTE TO THE READER: AS WITH ALL OTHER NEGATIVE EMOTIONS, LETTING GO OF OLD GUILT WILL NOT TAKE AWAY ONE'S ABILITY TO FEEL GUILTY IN THE FUTURE. THE READER IS ADVISED TO REMEMBER THAT TIME LINE THERAPY® DOES NOT TRANSFORM PEOPLE INTO UNFEELING ROBOTS. IF ANYTHING, IT INCREASES THE COMMUNICATION BETWEEN THE CONSCIOUS MIND AND THE UNCONSCIOUS MIND, CONSEQUENTLY CREATING A BETTER ENVIRONMENT FOR RIGHT BEHAVIORS AND DECISIONS.

One certainly does not need any lecturing to know that the past is the past and it cannot be changed. However, by changing the way we structure the meaning of past events and experiences, and by the integration of new and useful learnings, we can change the way we feel about ourselves in the present, and in the future. This method proves to be successful for a simple reason. Guilt (and shame) is contingent on time for the expression of its meaning. We can all remember times in the past when we made mistakes, some greater than others. Guilt was appropriate at that time. Maybe even shame was appropriate. We did something, we got caught, and we were ashamed. Simultaneously we began to feel guilty. Maybe it was something stupid, ridiculous, but we did not mean any harm. Maybe it was not even our fault. Maybe we thought we should feel guilty because others told us so. Now, after many years, that old guilt, although still present inside our neurology, is meaningless.

Another essential point to bear in mind is that without considering the element of time, negative emotions (guilt included) have no inherent meaning. They do not exist in the present. It may seem pointless to mention, but no negative emotions are floating around in the air wherever we are. Negative emotions from the past exist only in one's mind, and if this is the case, they are not of the present. They technically do not exist. The memory of an event is just that – a memory. The event has passed; it was finished a long time ago, and the only thing that remains are the memories of that event, stored in one's mind. It is also worth mentioning that it is a well-known fact that one's memories are notoriously inaccurate, and so, many people feel guilt for erroneous reasons.

NOTE TO THE READER: LET US REMEMBER THAT TIME LINE THERAPY® DOES NOT CHANGE MEMORIES. OUR MEMORIES DEFINE WHO WE ARE, AND, THEREFORE, IT IS NOT ADVISABLE TO REMOVE THEM. HOWEVER, WE CERTAINLY CAN CHANGE HOW WE THINK ABOUT THOSE MEMORIES, FROM A NEGATIVE, INTO AN EMPOWERING AND CONSTRUCTIVE PERSPECTIVE.

Change Is Not Mandatory

As exciting and inspiring as all this information may be, it is not a new concept. Over the last one hundred years alone, there have appeared many inspirational books and personal development trainings which, in one form or another, talk about the same thing. If one wants to change, one ought to begin with the inner world of emotions and beliefs. However, until today, to this author's knowledge, no other similar technique allows one to easily let go of past negative emotions to such a degree that they completely disappear, never to return.

Just about everyone has faced tough times at one point or another. Nonetheless, there are people who have faced severe challenges in their lives, challenges so serious that it begs the question of how is it possible for one human being to do such things to another human being? And yet, despite those challenges, there are many who have chosen to stop allowing excuses to slow them down. These people have decided that old problems will no longer hold them back or keep them stuck. They transformed the prison in which their mind was held, into a source of power, courage, and determination. These people serve as examples to the rest of us.

A few years ago, one of our coaching clients was convinced that his whole life was in a tailspin. But, after he realized that the self-pity trap is an incredibly boring and stuck place, he decided to get out of the confined mode of thinking. He learned new skills and began an acting career. Because he took this action, he got back on track rather quickly. Now, even with the economy dragging along, he is very successful. He is an embodiment of the old adage, "life is neither good nor bad; it is what one makes of it."

Those who take action have the most success in life, even when their actions sometimes turn out wrong. Without trying, we should have no right to complain about things not being the way we expect them to be. It is not fair or realistic to do nothing and expect things to change.

In conclusion, to make Time Line Therapy® techniques work, one has to really want to change. Just saying that one wants to change, but expecting that change will happen miraculously and without taking any action, will not help. In fact, it will just reinforce the belief that change is not possible.

Throughout the many years of doing seminars and trainings, we have encountered exceptions to the thousands and thousands of people who use Time Line Therapy® techniques successfully. For whatever reason, sometimes one needs to prove that it can work for everybody but him or her. They refuse to follow the instructions given and decide to keep their negativity. Evidently, this is a choice only one can make for oneself.

On the other side of this, for most people, there is no easy answer regarding how to change and what to change in life, even if they are not unhappy. Change can be uncomfortable, if for no other reason than its unfamiliar feeling and newness. And, there are plenty of people who live by the saying, "Better the devil you know than the one you don't."

W. Edwards Deming (1900-1993), who was an American consultant, statistician, and educator, wrote,

It is not necessary to change. Survival is not mandatory.[6]

We could translate this quotation into, "It is not necessary to change anything. Satisfaction and fulfillment at the end of life are not required." But if satisfaction and fulfillment do please the reader, s/he will be advised to consider what changes s/he must make now to break free from the cycle or pattern in which s/he is trapped.

Unfortunately, there are still too many people committed to creating permanent drama, failure, and disappointment, no matter what they do. It is not their fault. They do not know the difference. How changed could their lives be if they knew? It is hard to say for each individual person. However, with all of the empowering and inspirational books out there, with all the trainings, seminars, coaching and workshops available, we sometimes wonder if some people would prefer to take a seminar called "How to Become a Total Disappointment: A Practical Guide."

As previously said, it is not that one would do so purposefully. However, there is little chance of finding real fulfillment and satisfaction if one gets caught up in that trap.

NOTE TO THE READER: IT IS THIS AUTHOR'S EXPECTATION THAT THE READER HAS NOTICED THAT THE STATEMENTS IN THE "TEST YOURSELF" SECTION DO NOT REFER TO OTHERS

---

[6] "W. Edwards Deming." as quoted by BrainyQuote.com. Xplore Inc, 2016. http://www.brainyquote.com /quotes/quotes/w/wedwardsd377112.html

– THEY ARE ALL ABOUT YOURSELF.

✝ It is true that there exists a slight possibility that the changes one desires will occur independently, and without direct conscious intervention. The following are but a few small examples of wishful thinking which do not imply any action or responsibility.

"Maybe that gorgeous person you saw at that party will fall in love with you overnight, or your thoughtless boss will quit and leave you with her job."

"Maybe just by watching sports on your favorite television channel, by the power of osmosis, one morning you will wake up twenty pounds thinner and with a six-pack strong as steel." "Maybe an unexpected inheritance from a relative you never met will enrich your bank account by several million dollars."

"Maybe you might even wake up to another reality where you are younger, more attractive, richer, and a renowned movie star (if you care to be a movie star)."

Oh, and let us not forget, "You might win the lottery."

Slight and unlikely as they are, these are still actual possibilities. All right, maybe not the part about waking up in another reality. Yet, for most of us, such hopes may be pleasant daydreams during a hot summer day on the beach, but most of the time, they just are not going to happen. So, there is one way to ensure such success, and that is to take action and make it happen.

It Is a Matter of Choice

The first principle of positive change is that people who do not succeed tend to shift the responsibility for their lack of achievement onto others, or onto circumstances. The economy and even the government are also good to blame, followed closely by family, the weather, or any other thing over which they have no control. Some of these reasons for "Why my life is the way it is!" are ingenious, and a few of them are even justifiable by the facts. But, reasons cannot and will not help anybody find satisfaction, happiness, fulfillment, and financial or emotional wellbeing. So, why hang onto them?

In career and business, for example, the economy is the easiest thing to blame for one's lack of achievement. When you turn on the news and see that the economy suffered another hit, it is tempting to say, "How can I possibly do well when businesses everywhere are struggling?"

Then there are personal excuses, many of which were listed on the previous questionnaire, although, that list is by no means exhaustive. In years of training, we have heard lots of excuses and reasons, numerous times, in many countries and in many different languages.

At this juncture, the reader may expect a lecture about how unfounded those reasons are, however, admittedly, each of those excuses probably has some merit. The economy is not always at its best, and as of 2008, there are serious problems worldwide. Maybe the boss is a dull and unintelligent person, and the competition in the business is playing unfairly. Maybe the customers are having problems at home with their spouses, with their children, and with paying their mortgages and this is why they do not react well to your communication. Maybe it is hard to make decisions that could actually change one's life. Perhaps it requires too much courage and one just does not have that drive or that inner power.

Perhaps one merely has unrealistic expectations.

Yet, the techniques presented herein will not do anything **to** anybody. This is a significant difference in understanding. Many people are mentally trained to look for something to "make them better," not recognizing that the help cannot come from "out there" without any willingness to take action "in here." When asked about what Time Line Therapy® does for people to make them happy, here is what we tend to say "The techniques do not do things **to** you, but will work **with** you if you choose to use them."

All of the said factors, and our unresolved past negative experiences, added by the existence of limiting decisions and beliefs, prevent us from judging life´s situations correctly. As we have seen, negative emotions are primarily responsible for the gradual breakdown of the normal thinking process, which is essential for natural survival.

A disruption of positive thought patterns, over a longer period of time, affects not only the mind but also the body systems, to such a significant degree that even simple things seem to be unachievable. When that happens, people become insecure and begin to lack necessary self-esteem and self-confidence. They look up for approval and behave only as required so as not to upset anybody, and not to get in trouble.

Once in that position, they become hopelessly dependent on others. They have given their personal power away. Then, change becomes even more difficult, as in the process, they develop a "special" relationship and a set of benefits derived from their dependency. From here, the blame game is just a step away. Now it is the fault of the other when one is not given the approval one desires, but even if the approval is given, one still does not feel good enough, because the feeling is not present within. In these circumstances, one is literally stuck, insecure, and downright fearful.

The only thing that is really scary is the thought that fear can actually control us. The old adage, "The only thing to fear is fear itself." begins to make a lot of sense.

Taking Action

Here is where it gets complicated, because, despite of the wish to change something, one is drawn into finding many excuses to take no action at all. There is an expression which synthesizes this state of not taking action. It is when one "wants to want to" do something. In other words, one is decided, but the problem is when one arrives at the point of taking action. If one just wants to want to do something but is afraid of actually doing something, one will have a lot of reasons and justifications for not doing anything at all, because...

...that attractive person is most likely taken already. You saw her/him dancing with that handsome man/beautiful woman, and s/he probably does not want to be bothered by you.

...you do not have the time to go to the gym to workout, and furthermore, cookies and donuts taste so much yummier than fruits and vegetables. So, there is no reason to go through the hardship of improving your diet.

...you are not sure if you even stand any chance of getting hired for that excellent job, although you know very well that you are capable of doing it. So you do not even apply.

...there is no rich uncle in your family. You checked the family tree carefully.

...it is silly to believe in other realities, and anyway, movie stars also have complicated lives. It is all over the magazines.

...and who wins the lottery anyway? Those are unrealistic

expectations based on statistics.

Overall, action is what is needed the most. But to take action, one must first overcome the accumulated inertia. Thinking about changing things is easy; it is just a mental game. But many will look for all sorts of excuses not to take action; nevertheless, action is what makes things happen.

Some things are beyond your control, too. If they are, stop worrying about them. Forget about the things you cannot change, and worry only about those you can control.

Sometimes people find themselves in situations where they feel powerless. This happens precisely because they think, or they believe, that there is nothing they can do to affect any real change. Even then, there is always one thing that can be modified by the individual, and that is one's reactions to the environment. Admittedly, there is another little criterion that could help, and that is courage. One needs the courage to change oneself. One must find (1) the resolution to first admit that something is not working, after which (2) to recognize one's fears, anger, guilt, hurt, sadness, or other negative emotions, and then (3) proceed through the process of letting them go one by one. To let them go, they must be acknowledged, and that could be objectionable.

If we take a look at many of the world's sports celebrities, we could notice that some of them did not have a good start in life; maybe they came from single parent or guardian homes, from poverty or violent neighborhoods, or from third-world countries. Those are significant barriers. But, these people did not use their backgrounds or dysfunctional families as excuses; they made it to the top.

Admittedly, doing something new and taking a different course of action toward what you really want, involves, by the nature of its "newness," taking some risks. It requires stepping out of your comfort zone.

Let Us Talk Age

One common excuse for doing nothing is age. The old saying about not being able to teach an old dog new tricks is patently incorrect. It reinforces the belief that change is not possible, especially at an older age. However, as in our canine friend's case, people advanced in age, even if they may not learn as quickly as they did when they were young, can change behaviors and attitudes just as a younger person can. Maybe the adage about age and learning was not intended to serve as an excuse, but it is often used conveniently to reason one's way out of doing anything. Behavior is something learned, not something one is. Behaviors, like emotions, are not part of one's identity. They could become part of one's personality, but they are not who one is. It stands to reason then, that the other common saying of "This is just how I am, and there is nothing I can do about it" is equally as inaccurate.

If we liken one's identity to a marble statue, and each learned behavior was just a different cloth placed upon it, is it possible to change the sculpture? Unless extreme heat, chiseling or pressure is applied, probably not, or at least not without damaging it. But can one change or remove the cloth? The answer is yes, absolutely, and regardless of the age of the marble.

NOTE TO THE READER: YOUR IDENTITY IS NOT YOUR PHYSICAL BODY.

What is even more interesting, is that certain health problems that serve as an excuse could also be eliminated. Many health issues arise from negativity and unconscious stress, because as we know, mental health influences physical health. Developing a backache or a headache after a bad day at the office is a relatively common phenomenon. Instead of reaching for the pain medicine, one could realize that this is no more than mental stress creating physical pain. After letting go of unresolved negative emotions, many people have been told by doctors that their physical illnesses must have been misdiagnosed, because they could not have simply disappeared. Perhaps those diseases never existed in the first place.

There is a tremendous amount of power play and personal ambiguity bound up in unresolved negative experiences. These can be changed by turning those negative memories into sources of power and learning. Time Line Therapy® techniques are very good at helping one do that.

The Unconscious Mind

The techniques presented in the next chapters work with the unconscious mind. Therefore, we need to delve, albeit briefly, into the definition and functions of the unconscious mind. Although there are many different ways to describe the unconscious mind, from the perspective of Time Line Therapy® it is important to attempt to define it anew. The unconscious mind is the part of one's mind that is not directly under conscious control and which one does not experience directly. Think of it partly as an "autopilot" setting, in that it performs many processes we cannot perform consciously and yet it is doing this without any need of conscious control. The unconscious mind's job encompasses all the necessary things that make the body maintain proper functions and to which consciously, one does not have to pay any attention.

In fact, the unconscious mind is so much larger in its function and scope compared to the conscious mind that a sensible parallel would be to compare the electricity grid to a light bulb.

The term "unconscious mind" makes it sound as if it is a single thing, yet it fulfills many roles and duties in the body. We could simplify the concept by saying that the unconscious mind is the intelligence of the body, of which we are not consciously aware. It works continuously even while we are asleep. However, even by saying this, it is still difficult to pin down a clear-cut definition of the unconscious mind.

For example, think about the work that the body does to regulate the heartbeat. We do not consciously control it, and much of it is mechanical. But, when the unconscious mind detects danger, it can have a tremendous effect on the heart rate.

One scenario that could also partly describe a function of the unconscious mind could be, for example, if we are in a room with air conditioning, and we are not aware of it. Then, suddenly the air conditioning turns off. We may have only noticed the air conditioning after it turned off, although originally, we did not even notice that it was turned on. This is because, apparently, our unconscious mind was monitoring our surroundings and noticed the difference, while we were busy consciously paying attention to something entirely different.

Some people call the unconscious mind by other names like the subconscious mind. Others argue that it does not exist and that all we have is a cluster of conditioned reflexes. In some languages, the term "unconscious" does not even translate well. We agree that it is just a label. Nevertheless, it is important to keep in mind that, whatever we do call it, we need to recognize that there are underlying influences which control and fulfill many roles and duties in the complexity of our minds and bodies.

In the past, we had once a friendly discussion with two students who were also behavioral psychologists. They argued the point supporting their belief that there is no such thing as the unconscious mind, and that all we are dealing with are just conditioned reflexes. For the purpose of overcoming barriers and letting go of past obstacles, it really does not matter what we call it—the unconscious mind or conditioned reflexes. It is purposeless to argue semantics instead of being successful with eliminating barriers.

Even so, what if, by whatever means, we could change these underlying influences and conditioned reflexes to create positive change. What if, because of the changes allowed by Time Line Therapy®, we cold wake up feeling good, rather than grumpy? What if this could help people create positive behaviors, rather than continue with acting in ways that do not serve them? What if these methods could assist in creating instant change that is not arduous or difficult, and that lasts for a long time—if not forever? What could be wrong with that? Does it really matter if we call it the "unconscious mind" or "conditioned reflexes"?

✝ It comes as a surprise to many when they realize that not everybody thinks the way that they do, and that they're not always right. In fact, the notion of "right" becomes relative when, at the unconscious level, we deal with different situations. The unconscious mind does not rationalize in the same way as the conscious mind does. Evidently, there are basic moral considerations which are always right regardless of the circumstances, but if we put that aside, people have different motivations, which cause each individual to act or react, unconsciously, in a certain way. It does not mean that the unconscious mind is wrong, or some people are worse than others. Their behaviors may be inappropriate or plain wrong, but people themselves are not their behaviors. Nowhere is this more evident than in an unconscious "knee-jerk reflex" response, which, makes one respond in a certain way, often regardless of how they would prefer to act instead.

Simultaneously, once one begins to consciously understand that the behavior of one person, even if it is wrong, is not the person, one also begins to grasp that, as the cloth covering the marble piece, it can be changed. Then, the premise upon which to make a change becomes self-evident. With the right approach and techniques, one can change the automatic responses in the unconscious mind, and allow for change to occur. This does not mean we must put up with unacceptable behaviors. However, if who they are is not their behaviors, even if they might have done something wrong, those behaviors can be changed and with that, they could change for the better. In this way, things have a chance to shift in a positive direction during our relationship with them. Behaviors become easier to change when we choose to let go of negative emotions, limiting decisions, and limiting beliefs

⊹ The Unconscious Mind at Work

Regarding its functions, the conscious mind is to the unconscious mind, what the mouth is for the digestive system. We control the mouth, but we can only influence our digestive system if we are lucky, or trained in how to work directly with the unconscious mind. Our mouth makes it possible for many things to enter the body, but without processing those things through the rest of the digestive system, they would not be of much use.

We can give a lot of credit to the conscious mind; it is important for our rational thought. It is what makes the difference between animals and humans. So we can say that the conscious mind is the thinker, the rational and reasonable part of our makeup. The unconscious mind is different. To give credit to the conscious mind for the functions controlled by the unconscious mind, would be like giving credit to the rooster for the sunrise. Admittedly, that is a bit of an exaggeration. However, it serves to illustrate the point. We tend to give our rational thought process the credit for things that it does not do, like digesting food, beating the heart, circulating blood, improving the immune system (when stress disappears), storing long-term memories, providing energy, feeling emotions, as well as many other things.

The unconscious mind does not think, at least not in the way we think consciously. It has its own way of "thinking" which responds to, and communicates with, emotions and symbols (pictograms). Therefore, we can postulate safely that the unconscious mind is emotional and not rational. Even so, its functions are crucial for keeping us alive. According to a team led by Professor Gerard Hodgkinson of the Centre for Organizational Strategy, Learning, and Change, at Leeds University Business School,

> Humans clearly need both conscious and non-conscious thought processes, but it's likely that neither is intrinsically 'better' than the other.[1]

When people talk about the unconscious mind (and this includes what we learn at a Time Line Therapy® training), they are focusing on the aspect of the unconscious mind that responds to symbols in solving problems and taking directives. We tend to characterize it as a tremendous resource, but one that does not have the capacity, or the need, to think for itself all that well. This is normal. The unconscious mind is by definition un-conscious, or not conscious. In fact, there are many examples of people giving it inadequate directions and ending up with inadequate solutions. This is why we tell students to learn SMART goals (see the

[1] University of Leeds (2008, March 6). *Go With Your Gut -- Intuition Is More Than Just A Hunch, Says New Research.* ScienceDaily. Retrieved June 8, 2010, from http://www.sciencedaily.com /releases/2008/03/080305144210.htm

sections on "Planting Success in The Future" and "A Time Line Goals Experience").

Because Time Line Therapy® practitioners have many verifiable tales of clients having had dramatic breakthroughs affecting their happiness and wellbeing, we do not feel we push the limits very far when we say that Time Line Therapy® can create a dramatic improvement in one`s life – with the assistance of the unconscious mind. Time Line Therapy® techniques rearrange critical unconscious resources stored in what we call the time line, so that the unconscious mind can improve its ability to create new and more resourceful behaviors. Essentially, behaviors that are conducive to failure are unconsciously and automatically changed for other behaviors that encourage success, and all of that can happen spontaneously with the help of the unconscious mind.

This brings us to one of the most important things regarding the unconscious mind. We can influence and support the unconscious mind to do all sorts of things that we could never do with direct, conscious thinking. The conscious mind does not know exactly where every negative emotion is stored in the body, or where that limiting belief about not being good or capable enough resides. It just knows that it thinks this way. Therefore, it must rely on the unconscious mind to make the change regarding negative emotions and limiting beliefs, if any permanent improvement is to be achieved.

Nevertheless, the conscious mind can create the conditions to allow the unconscious mind to change this belief successfully. We believe that Time Line Therapy® techniques, because they work with both the conscious mind and the unconscious mind, are tools that can serve the purpose of creating those better conditions. The material we cover on negative emotions is the key to this.

Unconscious Mind as a Tool for Change

The unconscious mind is the key to change. Only those who have tried to change a habit consciously know how difficult it is. Yet, when that pattern is changed at the unconscious level, it disappears with ease. The better one understands the functions of the unconscious mind, the better one can use it for success and happiness. Here are some of the most important duties of the unconscious mind:

- **The unconscious mind is in charge of storing our memories.** This is not usually something one considers, but the storage of memories is not a function of the conscious mind. It is interesting to notice that digital memories are harder to remember compared to memories that are filled with some emotional content aside from the factual data. So, there are ways to improve one's memory by knowing how to access it from the unconscious reservoir. In the 1500s, Giordano Bruno talked about "memory palaces." These are just metaphorical inner rooms in a memory palace which, aside from the data itself, contain pictures, sounds, and feelings. A memory with emotional content is far more memorable than one with digital data alone.

- **The unconscious mind activates information, experiences, stored memories, and strategies for behavior because one cannot remember everything consciously at all times.** Imagine having to remember everything consciously all the time. Having all the memories of a lifetime at the same time in the mind.

- **The unconscious mind responds to suggestions and it**

does its best to carry them out, in its own way. This is why hypnosis works for people who have some sort of connection with their unconscious mind, while it does not work with people who are completely dissociated from the intelligence of their body (the unconscious mind). It is not necessary for the two minds to communicate and be aware of the connection with each other. In fact, for a long time, the unconscious mind was considered evil. As our animal part, it was automatically relegated to an inferior and primitive rank. Luckily, the trend is turning and we are beginning to accept that the unconscious mind is as important as the conscious mind, however with different functions, in the working together of our interconnected mind and body.

- **The unconscious mind is in charge of emotions** – and here is the crux of the matter. It is our feeling nature and, therefore, it does not process digital computer data. It is what makes the difference between human nature and machine. A machine could be much more intelligent than our conscious minds, and the processing power greater by orders of magnitude. But a machine, no matter how much it will try to "learn" emotions, will not be able to feel the same way as a human being. For some people who experience a lot of negative emotions, becoming machine-like may look like the solution to their life's problems. Although in one sense this may seem desirable, ultimately in the process, one would cease to be human.

What Lies Beneath

Most of the emotions we experience stem from the unconscious mind, which, as we have seen, is the domain of emotions. We all can feel emotions at the conscious level. However, their source of origin is not the conscious mind. One may not be fond of any emotions, or may say that emotions are silly and irrational. In a sense that is correct. Emotions are not rational. They have nothing rational within them. Emotions are feelings, not concepts, they do not run according to rational or scientific principles.

If the reader would like to try something right now, s/he can think about the last time s/he was angry. How much reason was in that emotion? The emotion of anger does not have reason in itself. The process of reasoning comes from the conscious mind, by attaching the anger to something or someone, but the emotion itself does not have reasoning. The last time we cheered our favorite sports team or hugged the person we love most in the world, we did not feel happy, loved, or satisfied following a reasonable or logical, conscious process. Even if we tried, logically it is impossible to feel anything. Logic is not feeling. If anything, many times it is anti-feeling.

No wonder it can be so hard to consciously change emotional patterns – one cannot directly control them with logic and reason. "I should not be angry right now" works only occasionally. That being the case, and since the unconscious mind is the source of all emotions, there is a great need for some sort of intervention for the instances when emotions seem to run amok. One way is chemical intervention. Change the chemistry and change the emotion. Unfortunately, the change in chemistry alone does not alter the actual emotion experienced in the original memory, or the event leading to the onset of the running-amok emotions. In other words, if the emotions on the original event are not released, without the chemical aid, the person would still feel the same old emotions. Regrettably, many techniques for changing emotions focus on logic and reason alone, and it could take many years to change an unconscious emotional pattern that way. With Time Line Therapy®, it takes an average of ten to fifteen minutes, or less, to entirely let go of one major negative emotion.

Not being the thinker, the unconscious mind is not always good at keeping negative emotions from interfering with our activities, reactions, and sleep patterns. This is because it instinctively knows that memories storing unresolved negative emotions are detrimental to the physical, emotional, and mental wellbeing. Once it stores emotions in a collection of memories around an individual subject, it tries to solve the negative ones because they are bothersome. In its own way, it does its best to relieve the body from constant and un-useful stress. The word "stress" in this context is used to represent negative emotions, limiting decisions, and limiting beliefs that block us, block our health, and block our general level of comfort in life. Therefore, it is recommendable that the negative feelings not be ignored, but rather than they be released. To do that, the unconscious mind needs to be instructed correctly and as we shall see, Time Line Therapy® methods purposefully guide the process of letting go by taking advantage of this natural function of the unconscious mind.

✚ The Battle between the Minds

This thinking may seem odd and unusual, and yet, new methods of coaching, and new discoveries in the fields of neurophysics, neurobiology, and neuropsychology confirm it, albeit in a new and scientific language.

We can safely assume that conventional beliefs about the unconscious mind are outdated. Regardless of the fact that Freudian theory has been discredited, many people still have no knowledge of the fact that at the unconscious level, we always feel the need to fix old issues, get completion on past events, and release old negative emotions.

This is an important concept to remember, especially during those times when there seems to be a battle going on between different motivations inside one's mind. To substantiate the notion that the unconscious mind wants to resolve issues from the past memories, consider some early morning dreams. It happens in those vague moments before waking up, when one is half-awake but yet, half-asleep, refusing to open the eyes in order to finish that last dream. Those strange images, semi-realistic scenarios that fill one's mind, full of metaphors and streams of seemingly non-related memories, are vented out by the unconscious mind through those early morning dreams. This is the unconscious mind's attempt to have a "house cleaning" moment. It happens randomly, in whatever priority of "cleaning" it chooses, and it is out of conscious control. In effect, the unconscious mind attempts to get resolution on past events and get rid of the negative emotions, limiting beliefs or limiting decisions accumulated on those old memories.

Time Line Therapy' techniques are a systematized duplication of this natural process, organized in a series of simple steps for the purpose of enabling one to tap into the unconscious venting process, as well as to use it with volition to achieve specific outcomes and results.

scious Mind Needs Direction

h mentioning another not-so-apparent piece of Our beliefs and decisions, including the limiting ones, are expressed with words. **Therefore, with the language and the words we use, we "instruct" the unconscious mind to respond in particular ways.** Time and time again, over the years, we have witnessed the presence of new words, or new meanings associated to words, all involved in telling us of "new" things about which to fear and panic. There is always something about to get us. We hear of these things, and many times, although we have no experience of "them" happening the way it was described, we respond automatically, thus unconsciously, and rush to the conclusion that we must be afraid. We forget that the information is presented through the lens of another person or institution, and, therefore, could be twisted, tweaked, inaccurate, or even false.

We are disposed to forget that what we see on television, and moreover on YouTube, could be photo-shopped, or cut and sliced into sound-bites. We forget that entertainment is not necessarily knowledge. Moreover, in the process of forgetting the said things, we also forget that we consciously instruct the unconscious mind to focus on negative things, paradoxically installing those things in the unconscious mind by auto-suggestion. And so we enter into a never-ending loop. If we consciously focus on scary things, and the language we use instructs the unconscious mind to feel negative emotions, we will experience more fear. And from here on, everything could get erratic, and the result could be perpetual fear and worry, in different degrees.

When one responds with a "knee-jerk reflex," unthinkingly, un-judgingly, and automatically, it is almost like a button is being pressed which elicits a particular reaction. Logic and reason seem to vacate the space for an emotional and almost childish response. There must always be a critical evaluation of the "input button," without which, we are left with an uncontrolled emotional reaction.

Here is a simple example presented for the purpose of noticing how easy it is to experience baseless negative emotions. Let us assume that one talks to one's neighbor who reports that at their son's school, one of the children got bitten by a stray dog. There are not many stray dogs around anymore, but for argument's sake, let us assume there is such a thing. Let us also assume that one receives this hearsay information, and unthinkingly, just reacts. One comes home already in a state of panic, calls over one's children and instructs them to look for stray dogs, hurry to fix the fence so no dogs could ever jump over it, and depending on how big the panic is, one may even feel compelled to call the school principal and make a big case of it.

Is there anything wrong with instructing the children to avoid interacting with stray dogs, or to fix the fence? Absolutely not. What is wrong is that one's reaction is not based on anything real that one could prove. The story was told by a neighbor who heard it from their child, who heard it from a group of children at school. Three levels of separation. Until more precise data and facts could be gathered, one could not even be sure whether this was a real story or some children wanting to be interesting. Nevertheless, the unconscious mind responded without conscious guidance, and created an automatic and baseless wave of negative emotions. It thought that perceived some danger, and it reacted to it. It is its job to do so. However, it is the conscious mind's job to feed the unconscious mind with the right information, so that unwarranted emotional responses are avoided.

We have seen that the role of emotions and, by extension, the role of the unconscious mind, is often greatly underestimated in the minds of most people. However, in the field of psychology, their importance is neither overlooked nor discarded. Psychologists know that emotions have a significant role in

> ...adaptively shifting perceptions, behaviors, and decisions.
> ...Examples of emotional influences on perception, behavior, and decision-making are well-known, yet much of this research has focused on detailed accounts of the proximate mechanisms through which emotions influence these phenomena. [1]

Since this is the case, it stands to reason that investigating and coming to terms with, i.e. letting go of, certain negative emotions, would result in real behavioral outcomes. If we combine this with the undesirable effects felt as a result of negative emotions, it becomes self-evident why working with the unconscious mind is so important. Therefore, if we are wise, we must pay attention to (1) recognizing our Negative Emotions, and the resultant Limiting Decisions and Limiting Beliefs, while (2) finding their source and (3) releasing what is impractical and unhealthy while maintaining all that is positive, which includes positive emotions, strategies, learnings, and new attitudes and behaviors.

---

[1] Martie G. Haselton, , UCLA, & Timothy Ketelaar, Center for Behavior Evolution and Culture New Mexico State University, Department of Psychology, *Irrational Emotions or Emotional Wisdom?, The Evolutionary Psychology of Emotions and Behavior,* p.10. In press, J. Forgas (ed.), *Hearts and minds: Affective influences on social cognition and behavior.* (Frontiers of Social Psychology Series). New York: Psychology Press., 8/18/2005, http://www.sscnet.ucla.edu/comm/haselton/webdocs/HaseltonKetelaar.pdf

How It Works

Before we begin the practical part of this book, we must say that Time Line Therapy® techniques use imagination. The techniques are fun, comfortable, and easy to do. Nonetheless, one must use imagination to make them work. They do not require any emotional effort or the re-living of distressing memories.

Time Line Therapy® works with "active imagination," which to begin with, helps the conscious mind to learn what resides in the unconscious mind. As long as we are unaware of the negative emotions stored at the unconscious level, we cannot begin the process of letting them go. By simply dissociating from them, it does not mean that negative emotions are not present. Dissociation, although a necessary phenomenon, if it persisted for a long time, could create even more problems. Moreover, the unspoken and often tricky part is to consciously begin to discover how to co-operate consciously with the unconscious responses of the (unconscious) mind.

Therefore, in Time Line Therapy® we use active imagination to follow the instructions given by someone else, **following a definite procedure and a precise series of steps.** For example, one of the things necessary is the ability to imagine floating above an imaginary time line. Therefore, one is supposed to imagine one's own time line, and also, imagine floating above this line. This is all done by active imagination. The time line is not real as in having substance. It is a mind concept. It requires that one imagines it, however one wants.

It is with imagination that one creates in one's mind a time line containing all of the memories from the past, all assembled together in a sequential way. These memories form a linear arrangement, a "time line" above which one is to imagine floating. The active imagination of the time line could be as a line drawn on paper, like a tunnel of light, as a series of slides which are the memories themselves, in color or black and white, or in any other shape or form. There are many different ways to imagine the time line, and they are all correct, because as previously discussed, the unconscious mind is symbolic.

Therefore, we can think of the time line as being a symbolic representation of all the memories put together. It is easy to imagine walking in a park, or on a beautiful beach. It is also easy to imagine oneself at home with family when one is actually at work. Similarly, one can imagine looking through the window from a very tall building and seeing the street below with the traffic of cars and pedestrians going by. Therefore, it stands to reason that one can also construct an imaginary time line of all the memories from the past, imagined, as if seen from above.

Regardless of the fact that Time Line Therapy® techniques work with active imagination, they produce real life results. If we sensibly consider this matter, we realize that the mind itself is not real in the same sense, which means that it does not have substance. Yet, what is present in one's mind, (1) is very true for that person and (2) determines one's behaviors and actions.

Active imagination has been used in psychology for many years, and it is well-known that even if something is only "in your head," it is also true in one's reality, much like the placebo effect.

Experiences of active imagination become rewarding and productive in real life because they translate into a change in behavior. In turn, these behavioral changes build creativity and inspiration for more positive change in the future, and there is nothing like creativity and inspiration to produce more motivation and better results.

The Basics

In Time Line Therapy® we part ways with traditional psychology in that we adopt a more quantum approach. We take into account that the whole body's neurology is involved in the experience and storage of emotions, not only the brain. Let us assume that emotions are not only stored in the brain, but in a holographic fashion, they are stored in every cell of the body. It follows then, that because negative emotions are stored in the same way, they have the ability to block the natural flow of energy, information, and the natural communication between those cells. The fields of quantum biology, as well as epigenetics[1] have demonstrated these said influences. Although, on the surface, the field of epigenetics does not take into account the internal environment, one famous biologist, Dr. Bruce Lipton[2] went so far as to demonstrate the connection between the "inner

---

[1] Epigenetics is the science of how environmental signals select, modify, and regulate gene activity ... The activity of our genes is constantly being modified in response to life experience which again emphasize that our perceptions of life shape our biology. Source: Bruce H. Lipton, Ph.D., *The Biology of Belief: Unleashing the Power of Consciousness, Matter, & Miracles.* 2008. Hay House, Inc 2008, p.xv

[2] Dr. Bruce Lipton is an American developmental biologist, author of *The Biology of Belief: Unleashing the Power of Consciousness, Matter, & Miracles* 2007, *Spontaneous Evolution: Our Positive Future and a Way to Get There From Here*, 2010, *The Honeymoon Effect: The Science of Creating Heaven on Earth*, 2014. Dr Lipton is the promoter of the idea that genes and DNA can be manipulated by a person's beliefs. His Ph.D. thesis was in Developmental Cell Biology, University of Virginia, Charlottesville, VA. With the title: *Myogenesis in Cell Culture: An ultrastructural study.*

environment", thus our beliefs, the expression of genes, and even DNA. Change the beliefs and, therefore, change the genes' expression and DNA. But quantum biology and epigenetics are too complicated, and this is a good reason to resort to something simpler, although no less effective, and that is Time Line Therapy®.

It stretches credibility to notice the amazing creativity and energy that flows from people after they release negative emotions. In many cases, it is indeed, incredible. It is also remarkable to see the physical, mental, and emotional wellbeing that results from this process. Therefore, the only logical conclusion is that at the very least, negative emotions deplete our bodies' resources. Whether we give free reign to negative emotions or struggle to suppress them, they absorb energy that we could put to better use. **In other words, negative emotions expressed or repressed, create the same effects.**

When we overreact and give free reign to our emotions, we can cause all sorts of problems, from road rage to unemployment, to high blood pressure and the like. When we underreact (suppress negative emotions), we are not asserting ourselves and handling situations as they arise, which can be costly and harmful. However, with negative emotions processed and eliminated, our vision and goals align with our highest values, making them achievable and much more enjoyable.

A Possible Scenario

Imagine for a moment the following scenario. Let us suppose that a person is having trouble meeting a deadline, mostly because of worries about not doing a good enough task and, therefore, s/he procrastinates. Somehow, this deadline has become a threat rather than a date on the calendar. The project must be completed and yet, s/he cannot get going. Possible dire consequences appear in her imagination, maybe based on past or even imaginary experiences, of not fulfilling said task by its due date. Some of the imaginary consequences are laughable, some are possible, but one outcome is inevitable. The project must be done timely. The more s/he thinks of possible negative consequences, the larger the thoughts grow, until s/he begins to feel anxiety. This is the process of making a mountain out of a molehill.

S/he knows that the project and the related tasks must be attended to as quickly as possible, but simultaneously, s/he fears what could happen if s/he actually does complete the project. What if the work is not going to be good enough and up to the required standard? Working on the project could mean failure for not doing a good-enough job. Not completing could also mean trouble. The boss will be unhappy either way. This person may not even realize it consciously, but the unconscious processes running in the background can turn a concern like this into an energy-depleting issue.

Because major negative emotions are only useful in the moments of fight or flight, or in an immediate need to avoid something life-threatening, this unconscious reaction is not helpful. Even if this hypothetical person were to reason and say, "Everything is fine – I can handle this." the body will still produce a physical stress response. It is wiser not to allow the body to react to imaginary threats and use its resources prematurely, just as it is unwise to be sweating and gasping for air while as one works on a task. Unless, of course, one is part of the club who enjoys an adrenaline rush, we definitely do not want our deadlines to turn into scary movies.

But let us follow our hypothetical scenario further along. The present worries of the deadline have now changed into fear, and that fear, in its turn, creates more negative unconscious expectations. In effect, this person has managed to insert (unconsciously) an adverse outcome into his/her future. Some pop psychology people refer to these negative expectations as self-sabotage or as self-fulfilling prophecies. Since the unconscious mind is so good at turning such expectations into realities, the negative outcome is likely to actually happen if one thinks it will.

This does not happen because of fate, but because this person's behaviors, influenced by the negative emotions, could naturally be leading to such an outcome. And here, we meet another important principle to remember. **A persistent pattern of thoughts in the unconscious mind has a considerable likelihood to happen, or to become real.** Therefore, based on past accumulated negativity, we also define and determine our future. Differently stated, the unconscious mind also defines the future based on its past emotional baggage. If the past is dominated by emotionally and negatively loaded images, then one's future will automatically proceed based on that set of presuppositions.

The net result is that, even if only unconsciously, one feels squeezed by fear from both the past and future. Worse yet, this fear may rise up in the present, about to pounce, giving orders and kicking for not getting the work done quickly enough. This stressful feeling is what happens when fear is pressing down on "the now," as a thumb squashing the person right on his/her time line.

The sensations, emotions, and unconscious imagery create a feedback loop that can get worse, especially because fear can worsen procrastination as well. Freedom from this kind of vicious cycle is very desirable. Even if a procrastination problem remains after this, it will be much easier to tackle when the events in the time line are positive and supportive. This hypothetical scenario is only one example of what a negative emotion (fear) can do to us.

In the section titled "Root Cause: Tapping Transformation," we will explain how the "root cause" of a negative belief or limiting decision (meaning the very first time when something of that nature happened), can become a source for present behaviors. Often, when something really intense happens, we make quick decisions that we do not remember consciously. We might be aware later on that we have that belief. Nevertheless, we do not remember its moment of inception consciously.

Let us take another example. Two young children are at school, and during a test, they do not perform as well as they wanted. The teacher, wanting to be encouraging and motivating says to both, "You're just not good enough at this thing!" One of them may unconsciously decide to accept this and from there on believe that s/he is not good enough. The other one may say, "Of course I am good enough, and I will prove it on the next test!"

Although the first child may not remember consciously making that decision, it will influence him/her in the future. Once established, a decision or a belief will remain steadily lurking in the unconscious mind, until such time one chooses to change it. But even then, a conscious decision i.e. "From now on I won't believe this anymore." is not enough. The belief has to be let go from the unconscious mind. In fact, the unconscious mind is the primary place where change must occur.

For that reason, past decisions and beliefs that do not serve us unconsciously run our lives, and in the process they become interwoven with patterns of negative emotions to form a strong string of limitation.

Even if we do not remember many of those events consciously, and usually we do not, the emotions, decisions, and beliefs continue to affect us throughout most of our lives. They seem to appear at the most inopportune moments and, in many instances, erect barriers, where we could otherwise take advantage of many opportunities. This is why, for most people, simply becoming aware of these emotions, decisions and beliefs is not nearly enough. They must be eliminated, if we really desire to make a worthwhile change to the way we unconsciously, and therefore automatically, respond to life events and situations.

The information we have just reviewed about negative emotions and limiting decisions is enough for doing the first process. Next, let us experience the first technique in Time Line Therapy®.

The Inspired Time Traveler

From this section on, we will address the reader directly since it contains directions for working with Time Line Therapy® techniques. If so chosen, the reader can follow the instructions and the steps to discover how s/he stores time, and how to utilize the time line to let go of negative emotions, limiting decisions and limiting beliefs.

Imagine what could be accomplished if one could travel through time. This theme preoccupied brilliant human minds for centuries if not millennia. The theme of time travel has been contemplated by H. G. Wells[11] and Isaac Asimov[12] who were two great writers and visionaries of this future possibility. However, until physical time travel becomes a reality, we can travel in time in our minds as a method for further development.

NOTE TO THE READER: LETTING GO OF NEGATIVE EMOTIONS, LIMITING DECISIONS AND LIMITING BELIEFS IS, IN FACT, AN

---

[11] H. G. Wells, was a prolific English writer in many genres, including the novel, history, politics, and social commentary, textbooks and rules for war games. Wells is now best remembered for his science fiction novels, and is called the father of science fiction, along with Jules Verne and Hugo Gernsback. His most notable science fiction works include The Time Machine (1895), The Island of Doctor Moreau (1896), The Invisible Man (1897), and The War of the Worlds (1898). Source: https://en.wikipedia.org/wiki/H._G._Wells

[12] Isaac Asimov was an American author and professor of biochemistry at Boston University, best known for his works of science fiction and for his popular science books. Asimov was prolific and wrote or edited more than 500 books Asimov wrote hard science fiction and, along with Robert A. Heinlein and Arthur C. Clarke, he was considered one of the "Big Three" science fiction writers during his lifetime.Asi mov's most famous work is the Foundation Series; his other major series are the Galactic Empire series and the Robot series. Source: https://en.wikipedia.org/wiki/Isaac_Asimov

EXCELLENT TOOL FOR PERSONAL DEVELOPMENT AND INCREASED PRODUCTIVITY. IT IS ALSO A TOOL FOR ENHANCING CREATIVITY AND IMAGINATION, BOTH VERY USEFUL FOR FINDING SOLUTIONS TO MANY OF LIFE'S PROBLEMS AND DILEMMAS.

In the next section, the reader will be taking a significant step toward becoming a kind of time traveler. S/he will learn how to travel with his/her mind's internal time machine, which we call the time line, in order to create desirable changes in health and success. Fortunately, it feels great to apply these skills and learn these insights.

The next chapter will begin to discover how one stores time. Once the reader becomes accustomed to what kind of time traveler fits his/her thinking, s/he will be able to apply Time Line Therapy® techniques so that it fits the manner in which s/he organizes his/her time line. It sounds like a lot right now, but by going through the theoretical chapters slowly, it is easy to figure it out. We will keep it short and simple.

One's unconscious mind organizes events in the past in such a way that they are accessible chronologically, and this has been the subject of recent studies. In September 2009, the BBC NEWS reported this from University of Edinburgh psychologist Julia Simner:

Imagine [...] time laid out in front of you, or surrounding your body. And you could physically point to specific dates in space. And that you may use the experience, unconsciously, every day. [...] Important dates might stand out – birthdays, anniversaries. And you could scan a visible timeline to check if you were available – whenever you made plans. No actual diary necessary.[13]

We agree. One can "see" time by using imagination, inside one's mind. Given that the memories are stored inside one's mind, and they do not exist as a solid reality, the way to access them and do the necessary modifications is also in the same place, in the "internal environment."

One thing before we proceed is that some people "feel" or "sense" their time memories, and with them their time line, while others "hear" them. A small number of people can even "smell" them. Most people, though, use pictures and movies played on their internal screen as they close their eyes. However, we need to remember that not everybody imagines with pictures. Regardless of the way one imagines things, everybody can do Time Line Therapy®, with either of the main three: pictures, feelings, or sounds.

Time Storage

We relate to time through our language, which uses verb tense to tell us what was in the past, what is in the present, and will be in the future. Something that "was" is as obviously something from the past as something that "is" evidently something happening in "the now", and something that "will be", of course, refers to the future. This is how we relate to time at a conscious level. However, the unconscious mind has its own way of accomplishing the same process regarding time.

---

[13] Victoria Gill, (2009). Can you see time? BBC NEWS. Retrieved from: http://news.bbc.co.uk/2/hi/science/nature/824859.stm

Instructions to the Reader

Think about something that you are planning to do tomorrow, something easy. Do you know what you will have for breakfast? Will you be cooking something? Will you go to a drive-through for breakfast? Maybe you will have some bran flakes and a cup of raspberry yogurt. No matter what it is, think of the food you will eat, and once you do that, think of the picture you have in your mind representing tomorrow's breakfast, even if it is just a cup of coffee or tea. Notice how it looks, feels, sounds, and smells.

Once you have imagined that, think about something similar you did earlier today or yesterday.

How can your mind tell the difference? You do not "just know" when each event happened and in which order. It may not be immediately apparent, but there is a particular process of organization used by the unconscious mind to help you do this.

Where is Your Past?

Most people organize memories in time by placing them in an imaginary space around them. For some people, the future may be off to the right, and the past may be off to the left. Other people have this reversed, with the future to the left and the past to the right.

On the other hand, many find that the future is out in front, and the past is behind. Both possibilities assume that the person is "in the now" as a moment in time. Perhaps this is why some people say, "I want to put this behind me." After all, that is where it belongs for them. Some people could say, "I see my future over there, to the left of me."

Instructions to the Reader

It is important to discover how the mind encodes things memory by memory. There is no "wrong" or "right" way of doing this. Allow your unconscious mind to create the symbol most suitable for you.

NOTE TO THE READER: THE UNCONSCIOUS MIND IS SYMBOLIC AND HOWEVER IT SYMBOLIZES THE TIME LINE IS CORRECT. REMEMBER THAT THE TIME LINE IS NOT "REAL", AS IN HAVING SOLIDITY, BUT A SIMPLE MIND CONSTRUCT.

What does a single memory appear like in your time line? There are many possibilities. Some people see the memories like frames on a film, so that when they want to fully experience a memory, it is a little like entering into that frame of the movie. Others see each moment like a slide in a stack. Do you remember slides? They were small transparent pictures that could be projected onto a screen, and you could pick a slide from anywhere in the stack. Some people do not see any memories at all; they just experience a "knowing" that the future is in "this" direction and "over there," in the other direction, is the past. Some people, who do not have a good visual imagination, feel their time line. For them, the memories are based on feelings, and those feelings cause other memories to come to the central point of attention. All these possibilities are correct.

How Emma Found Her Time Line

Emma could be the poster girl for making it hard to discover one's time line. For most people, imagining is a natural thing to do. Children imagine often – they find it easy – but for a small number of persons, the conscious mind's analytical function takes over the imagination, which makes it difficult.

Initially, when we asked Emma where her past was, she started analyzing the whole concept with a lot of analytical, left-brained rationale. "Well, if my past would be somewhere, it would be in Albany, NY ... And after that, I moved to North Carolina, and now I live in Chicago..." Finally, exasperated with her conscious search of something that she was supposed to imagine, she said, "I don't know where my time line is."

We asked her to imagine it being in some direction to or from her body, and she said, "But I feel that I'm making it up!" it could not be that easy!

With these words, Emma discovered the whole "secret" of how to determine one's time line.

Once she understood that she was supposed to imagine it and that however she imagined it was correct, she was immediately capable of pointing in two different directions from her body: ahead and to the right for her future, and behind and to the left for her past. For the first time, she discovered how she stored time at the unconscious level.

NOTE TO THE READER: TIME LINE THERAPY® INVOLVES A

PROCESS OF ACTIVE IMAGINATION. THEREFORE, IT FOLLOWS THAT ONE IS SUPPOSED TO IMAGINE IT. IMAGINATION PRESUPPOSES MAKING IT UP. IT IS A PROCESS OF IMAGINATION, AND IMAGINATION IS NOT SOMETHING ONE CAN TOUCH. IN EFFECT, WE ACTUALLY CONSTRUCT THE TIME LINE IN OUR MIND.

FURTHER NOTE TO THE READER: A VERY IMPORTANT POINT TO REMEMBER IS THAT ONE CANNOT IMAGINE SOMETHING THAT IS NOT CORRECT OR ACCURATE FOR THAT PERSON. EVEN IF ONE MAKES IT UP, IN OTHER WORDS, IMAGINE IT, PARADOXICALLY, ONE IS MAKING IT UP SOMETHING, HOWEVER THAT SOMETHING IS CORRECT *FOR HIM OR HERSELF* SINCE THE IMAGINATION ITSELF COMES FROM ONE'S OWN UNCONSCIOUS MIND.

THAT IS TO SAY, ONE'S IMAGINATION IS A REPRESENTATION OF WHAT RESIDES IN THE UNCONSCIOUS MIND. THEREFORE, IT STANDS TO REASON THAT ONE CANNOT MAKE UP INACCURATE REPRESENTATIONS. THE UNCONSCIOUS MIND MOLDS THE IMAGINARY CONSTRUCT FROM THE UNCONSCIOUS LEVEL, WHETHER ONE IS AWARE OF IT CONSCIOUSLY, OR NOT.

In Time, or Through Time?

Getting to know one's time line is like having a map of one's town; it helps one get around while using Time Line Therapy® techniques. Let us begin by advising the reader to find out whether s/he is an In-Time person or a Through-Time person.

1 - "In Time" time line

In-Time people have a time line that runs through their body with the future in front and the past behind them. The present is where they are now. The time line runs through them and it intersects with the body in the present moment.

As In-Time people move through life, the future connects with them and falls back into the past. A parallel could be done if one were to drive on a freeway in a car. If one imagines the freeway as the time line the car is always the "now" moment.

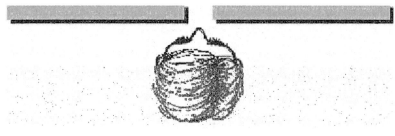

2 "Through Time" time line

Through-Time people experience their time line as a series of moments that do not run through the body. Generally, the memories are all out in front of them.

Most Through-Time people have their time line out before them, moving left to right with the "now" moment in the middle. This might resemble a history time line from a textbook or website.

But what if one's time line does not look like any of these two examples? For some people, the future can be in front and to the left, with the past in front and to the right, and with the "now moment" right where the person is. In this case, the time line makes a V-shape. Some time lines are curved or bent in different directions. Some time lines are straight up above the head for the future, with the past going straight down through the body. None of these possibilities are either right or wrong. Since it is a process of active imagination, it all depends on how much fun the unconscious mind had while constructing it.

Instructions to the Reader

If you have not discovered the shape of your time line yet, here are some ideas as to where to look. So far, we have been limiting the organization to spatial placement, but that is not the only way to organize time. As you think about memories of the past and plans for the future, notice if you have other, additional ways of organizing them for time. Many other examples would be possible, but to discuss other possibilities here would be beyond the scope of this book. As long as you imagine your time line in a way that you can tell the present, past, and future apart, you are doing a good job.

To find the direction of your time line, ask yourself this question, "If I were to know in which direction is my past and point to that direction, to which direction would I point?"

NOTE TO THE READER: IT IS CRUCIAL THAT YOU POINT RATHER QUICKLY. THE WRONG THING TO DO IS TO SIT AND ANALYZE THE CONCEPT. THAT IS WHAT THE CONSCIOUS MIND WOULD BE TEMPTED TO DO. HOWEVER, TO DISCOVER HOW YOU STORE TIME AT THE UNCONSCIOUS LEVEL, YOU MUST POINT QUICKLY. THERE ARE ONLY A FEW POSSIBILITIES. IN FRONT, TO THE BACK, TO THE RIGHT OR TO THE LEFT, UP OR DOWN. CHOOSE VERY QUICKLY, AND GO FOR THE ONE YOU INSTINCTUALLY FEEL.

Then ask yourself the same question for the future. "And in which direction would I point for the future?"

Once you have established the two directions, imagine a line uniting the past and the future. It does not have to be a straight line, it could be V shaped, or curved. Depending on how your time line is oriented, you may be a very organized and "timely" person, or a laid back and laissez faire person.

Jacob and Sam's Time Line Clash

Sam is the kind of person who always remembers everyone's birthdays and anniversaries. She is always planning ahead of time, and she could reel off the events coming in the next few months, including precisely where she would be going, and what she was going to do on each day of her vacation.

She remembered the smallest details of her daily tasks in advance, had reminders popping up regularly on her phone, and once she went to a new place, she never had to look up the address again. Her daily routine was extremely well planned and organized. She never missed an appointment and she got a lot done during the day. She is a very reliable person.

Jacob is her partner of fourteen years. Jacob goes to the store to buy groceries and inevitably forgets to buy the steak or the milk, and has to go back. He is fashionably late to appointments, virtually laissez-faire and very creative, but messy and disorganized. He also gets a lot done, but in his own time, and usually just before deadlines.

When they go on vacation, he just wants to do whatever he feels like doing in the moment, whereas Sam has everything programmed to the minute. They drive each other crazy. Neither one can understand why "the other" cannot be more organized or more relaxed.

The difference is just in how they store time. Jacob's time line runs through him from front to back, and Sam's time line runs in front of her from left to right.

Once they found out about the Through-Time vs. In-Time storage, they decided that they could be flexible and change their time lines according to their needs and circumstances. While at work and during the week, they put their time lines in front of them, and during the weekends on holidays, they change their time lines to be front to back. In this way, there were no more arguments, work was done effectively, and they both could really relax and enjoy their weekends and holidays together. They have the directions of their time lines to thank.

In-Time Has Plenty of Time

Let us look at how In-Time and Through-Time people experience time in real-life situations, and what this means to our behaviors. It may surprise the reader to find out that not everybody has the same relationship to time as s/he does. Some people who are exactly the opposite compared to you may even be annoying. Moreover, different ways of storing time extend not only to individuals and organizations. Whole cultures have been determined to have unique ways of organizing time, as well. When a vast majority of people in a culture code time in a certain way, it reflects that entire culture's relationship with time.

In-Time cultures can have trouble adapting to the time-bound industrialized and post-industrialized cultures, because "the now" is so dominant, that it overshadows the kind of planning demanded by the industrial or information era, which is particularly important in business situations. People living in "the now" usually have no sense of urgency, no need to get anything done, no need for completion, because as far as they are concerned, there is no past and no future—only a gigantic now-moment. This can be a blessing or a curse, depending on the situation.

If one is by nature a truly In-Time person, one probably does not do well when pressured by time constraints typical for the "westernized" type of time environment. One may feel endlessly frustrated, pressured, or barraged by the multi-tasking and butting-in that occurs. Imagine a sales person with no need for closure. Sales would never get done. This could lead to a lot of confrontations, non-performance, stress, and that poor sales person could end up feeling the need to tear his/her hair out.

Many Westerners have had to learn to adapt when they attend business meetings in In-Time cultures. This author had an experience where she had to wait for a considerable amount of time because the people with whom she had the meeting were not available until their prior arrangement was over, regardless of the time of our appointment. The meeting time was just a general reference point, like a lighthouse, not like a stopwatch at the starting of a race. In fact, the stopwatch never started.

Moreover, the long adjacent and non-related discussions also took a lot of time, and a meeting that could have been finished in one hour took just about four hours to complete. In situations like this, a person who is not In-Time, better learn to adjust their agendas as things fly along.

We were supposed to have the meeting at ten in the morning, but we were told that if they did not show up by eleven, we could have lunch at noon, and if after that time they still did not arrive, we could go have a coffee in the cafeteria. Eventually by three in the afternoon, they showed up and we finished out the discussion at dinner. There was no plan, no notes, and no organization for that meeting although it was supposed to contain business plans for the future. It had no strategies for marketing or advertising, no precise dates, but a very warm and fuzzy feeling about it. It was a fun time, though! In a true In-Time sense, there is nothing wrong with this model.

One particular boat captain, with a large cargo and a ship that was expensive to staff and operate, was having a terrible time getting inspected so that he leave the harbor. The person in charge of the harbor kept giving times for inspection, and those times kept passing without an actual inspection taking place.

The boat captain was not used to such procedures, and as a good Through-Time person, finally got so infuriated that he demanded to be given an exact time and date. After some detours, the representative finally gave him an exact time, and the captain yelled, "Definitely?" "Yes," was the reply, "Definitely ... um....probably...? I am sure that maybe... um... that is the correct time."

Through-Time is Always Urgent

A Through-Time culture, like the typical western culture, views time in more of a lock step, policy-directed, future-oriented and precisely-organized way. Time is full of deadlines. That is a source of power as well as a curse. Some of us thrive on it while many are overwhelmed and feel like we belong on another planet. If one is not well adapted to Through-Time, people with half that person's brainpower can run circles around him/her at work and make that poor person look like s/he is less capable, which is most likely incorrect.

Through-Time cultures are goal-oriented and very time aware. Every minute counts. There are only so many hours in the day and there are so many things to be done. One needs to rush to get everything done in a timely manner. Therefore, time is precisely organized, that there is no minute to lose to distracting activities.

Although Through-Time people tend to be high achievers, eventually they need to learn to relax, otherwise, eventually, they will succumb to stress and pressure. In large corporations, it is becoming rather popular to find meditation and quiet rooms. This is the place where, at least for a pre-determined period of time, a Through-Time person can become In-Time, and relax his/her mind.

In-Time people in a Through-Time world may need to transform their time-experience in some way. Some can do this well enough just by being selective in choosing a suitable career. Many, however, also need to do some change in their time lines so that they can adapt. This does not mean giving up your preferred style; it just means being able to switch when Through Time is called for.

How to Change the Time Line

It may not be immediately apparent, but we can change the how we construct time at the unconscious level. The process of changing the time line itself could be useful if we want to change how we relate to time. This process encourages your time line to respond better to your future goals and objectives, and it can help you overcome serious problems relating to time.

Instinctively, we seem to know the direction in which our time line feels most comfortable. Occasionally, we could experience the need to straighten it out. In general, the concept of the time line is something few people are concerned with and yet, it seems to have significant input in our personality and how we relate to time.

Is the Time Line Working Well?

The next step after we discover the natural orientation of our personal time line, is to consider whether it is working for our purpose, or against it. It is evident that for a person who works in a corporation, an In-Time time line is not desirable and could bring about difficulty.

Therefore, sometimes it is helpful to rearrange the time line from a position which diminishes our strength, to a place where it is most resourceful. We can adjust its location and position to best suit our momentary needs and circumstances. Then later, as our needs change again, there is nothing to prevent us from changing the direction and location of the time line back to where it feels more natural.

NOTE TO THE READER: THIS PROCESS IS MOST USEFUL FOR BUSINESS AND OTHER PERFORMANCE RELATED MATTERS. IT IS NOT DESIGNED TO BE USED AS A SOLUTION FOR TRAUMATIC EVENTS FROM THE PAST. DO NOT ATTEMPT TO SOLVE MEDICAL CONDITIONS WITH TIME LINE THERAPY®. CONSULT A HEALTH CARE PROVIDER FOR ADVICE AND TREATMENT.

Instructions to the Reader

Take a couple of minutes to experience your time line, in whichever way you imagine it. Be sure that it is clear enough to tell whether it goes through you or not. Make a mental note of where it is so that you can remember its original orientation and put it back later.

Now ask your unconscious mind to temporarily arrange your time line so that your In-Time (front to back) time line becomes a

Through-Time (right to left or left to right) time line, or vice versa. Imagine it changing direction and settling in a new place. Make this more of an invitation than a command to your unconscious mind, and wait for a minute, steadily extending the invitation to your mind to switch the orientation of your time line.

This is a simple process. Will it to move the other way, while at the same time, with your imagination, see it shift to the new desired location. If the time line does not move, remember that (1) you are making it happen through your imagination, and it is possible that (2) you may not know how to imagine it in a different way. Therefore, (3) imagine giving it a nudge. You can also remind your unconscious mind that there is no reason for alarm, that this is only temporary; you'll be changing it back after your exploration of the options. Remember, this is a process you do in your imagination, so changing the direction of your time line should be very easy to do. Just imagine it differently.

Now, take ten minutes to do something in your new time line, trying to stay aware of anything new in your behavior.

(1) If you just changed your time line to Through-Time, make a To Do list. Make a phone call that is urgent, or make one that you wanted to make but have not because it just was not urgent enough.

(2) If you changed your time line to In-Time, look at your already existing To Do list, and see if you have the same urgency as before. Maybe you think, "Oh, I have plenty of time to do it all—no rush!"

If it is appropriate, and if you would like to experiment a little more, you can let your time line stay in the new location for thirty minutes or longer in order to actually experience how it influences you. Later on, from these two choices, decide which is the most attractive according to your needs. Are you dealing with unfinished tasks and disorganization? You may want to leave your time line in front of you, from left to right. Are you too time aware on the weekends or in vacation? You may want to switch it to In-Time for those occasions.

Which one is the one you are most likely to need right now? Do you feel like you finally want to make that urgent call, which you should have done a week ago? Or, do you feel like you are always rushing and that there is no reason to do so?

After you have examined these options, you can consider whether the most appealing choice matches your current time line, or not? In other words, does it match your In-Time or Through-Time needs? You can get really playful with it and change it every day or even change it twice or more in the same day. After all, that playful spirit can juice up your creativity for better solutions and more motivation!

When you are done with this activity, remember to repeat the beginning of the exercise; only, this time, put your time line back to the way it was if you choose to do so.

Now you know your time organization (In-Time or Through-Time), and how to be more flexible, strategic, and creative in your relationship with time, projects, people, and recreation. This is the beginning of working with your time line. And this, tool is designed to take you even beyond these abilities.

To be in control of how you relate to time, is to be in what we call the Inspiration Zone. That is the place in which you are neither at war with time, nor afraid of the lack of time.

Time Struggles - Fear of Time

Some people are secretly afraid of time. One could say that time also holds many "black bags" of unresolved stuff. We are talking about bothersome events, traumatic memories, overwhelming experiences, and things we are not even supposed to think about, which we could call the forbidden zones.

These accumulated deposits of unwanted negative emotions, or for some, "personal history plaques and merit badges" interfere with achieving success in one's career, relationships, family, and life in general. If there is any kind of repeating pattern in one's life that holds that person back, or sabotages love, career, money, or anything else that is important to him/her, then the odds are very good that we will find the root of the problem in the past.

To begin the process of letting that emotional baggage go, first one needs to be willing to acknowledge its presence.

If it is too much to do here, and since this is not the complete set of techniques from Time Line Therapy®, at least, the reader will have an excellent idea of what s/he could do together with a Time Line Therapy˙ practitioner or coach to fix the problem. Another possibility is to learn to do it for oneself, but this is a longer process. In any case, discovering "fear from the past" is an important step.

Another kind of time-fear has to do with fear of the future. If one is afraid of some possible or even inevitable thing in the future, and if this fear distracts the person from being at his/her best, most likely, the roots of that future fear, still reside somewhere in the past.

Many people are at war with time, and they are rather public about it, yet they have never thought about it in this way. These people at war with time are often highly successful, unlike those who have fear-based problems that interfere with success. That war with time may even be a part of their success strategy. However, in the long run, if there are too many "black bags" of unresolved stuff from the past, eventually the physical body will give signs of stress, and we all know where too much stress could lead.

The War against Time

Here is an example of a man who experienced this "war against time" indirectly. His work involved re-upholstering waiting room chairs in the office of heart doctors. The man explained to the doctors that he found it unusual that the chairs were worn down on the front edges of the seats, instead of on the more common back area. The doctors, Meyer Friedman[1] and R.H. Rosenman, had been thinking about the fact that so many of their heart patients had "intense" personalities, and this oddity with the seats switched on a light bulb for them both.

Through-Time People often tend to live their whole lives on "the edge of the seat!" Once the connection was made, Friedman and Rosenman began to study the psychological risk factors for heart ailments, and decided that impatient, time-conscious, edge-of-your-seat personalities fit what they called a "Type A

---

[1] Meyer Friedman (July 13, 1910–April 27, 2001) was an American cardiologist who developed, with colleague R.H. Rosenman, the theory that the "Type A" behavior of chronically angry and impatient people raises their risk of heart attacks. The cardiologist and researcher worked until his death at 90 as director of a medical institute that bears his name.   Friedman, who often characterized himself as a "recovering Type A," and colleague Dr. Ray Rosenman began to write about the link between behavior and heart disease in scientific papers during the 1950s. They turned their observations into a popular 1974 book, "*Type A Behavior and Your Heart.*" Source: https://en.wikipedia.org/wiki/Meyer_Friedman

personality." Initially, the concept was rejected by the medical community. However, ultimately, it took root and was gradually embraced by the popular culture, where "Type A personality" became a buzzword. Friedman was of the opinion that personalities cannot be changed, and all we can hope is to try for more B-like behaviors.

With a change in the orientation of one's time line, and by releasing negative emotions, limiting decisions and limiting beliefs, one could change one's personality. In the book *Time Line Therapy and The Basis of Personality*,[1] we can find a demonstrated case of direct correlation between personality and the direction and organization of the time line.

Although Type A personalities are often higher achievers, sometimes the accumulated stress can create health conditions. They are sometimes called "stress junkies." At least, this was Friedman and Rosenman's conclusion.

In Time Line Therapy®, we take this to mean that it is the content of the stress that is the problem. Therefore, we suggest that the reader reads thoroughly the section that describes stress. The content of the stress (meaning the negative emotions, limiting decisions and limiting beliefs) could create the undesirable health effects; not the active and highly motivating life-style. Therefore, it is probably a good idea to get rid of this extra stress and preserve the motivation.

Through-Time without Break

---

[1] James, Tad and Woodsmall, Wyatt. Time Line Therapy and The Basis Of Personality. Copyright ©1988 by Meta Publications. Meta Publications. 1988. ISBN 0-916990-21-4. ISBN 978-0-916990-21-3

We all experience stress in our daily routines. Unless we leave to go and live in a cave, to meditate and avoid interacting with the rest of society, we have to deal with this stress. Therefore, it is safe to assume that whenever one puts oneself in demanding situations, one will accumulate stress. This is why it is advisable to, at least, let go of the stress from the past, as well as to do maintenance through a regular "house cleaning" process. It is especially beneficial if one is in a one-person race against time where one gets easily frustrated by obstacles. Moreover, when one is really stressed, one can end up projecting all this frustration onto other people, who can then become extra sources of stress, even if that happens only in one's mind.

Unfortunately, if a person gets in such a situation, things do not stop here. In general, people resent being targets for antipathy and dislike, and they may, in turn, decide to ramp up the stress by isolating the poor person. Some people will go very far to get angry with the people who do not cooperate with their time war. Stress accumulates and can create undesirable health effects.

On the positive side, without the extra stress, and with a method to relieve it, Through-Time people can be quite efficient at getting things done. In fact, even when they encounter health problems, they tend to be much more aggressive about doing everything their doctor recommends than the more laid-back In-Time people. After two heart attacks, Dr. Friedman did just that, and became a Type B in the process. He was actually the first to show, without Time Line Therapy®, that people can change their personalities even though his theories have been criticized.

In-Time Take a Break

In-Time people, or to use Friedman's categorization, Type B individuals, are more patient, relaxed, and easy-going. They do not have any sense of urgency. Their philosophy in life is straightforward. Since there is always plenty of time for everything, why rush to get anything done? Because of these characteristics, In-Time people do not get things done, are slow in producing discernable results, and are often apathetic and disengaged.

The Type B personality, or In-Time person, is the norm in society. It is the average person without any extra stress. These people are usually calm, and it takes a lot to irritate them. In-Time people do not have a problem driving behind a slow car, where as a Through-Time person would probably find themselves in agony. In-Time people also do not care too much if the line is long at the grocery store. Their pace is relaxed and they are at peace with being slow(er).

A combination of In-Time and Through-Time, according to one's daily needs, could provide more balance. Switching the direction of the time line takes a few minutes, and if one choses to change it contextually, one can be as productive as needed but still have the ability to relax as desired. When these time disruptions – the fear of time and the war against it – are resolved, one could become more dynamic than before, and have the confidence and peace of mind that one can relax when needed, while maintaining a healthy body and mind.

The Future

We have addressed many issues related to things that accumulate in our memories from the past, and how they could create stress and discomfort ultimately culminating with possible health problems. Even when we discuss the future, we seem to face similar situations. Nevertheless, as we begin talking about the future, we need to mention the obvious. **The future has not happened, yet! It is ours to create with every decision and choice that we makes, every day.**

Many people color their future with fears that stem from past experiences. Others even envisage the worst possible scenarios, even if they are only imaginary. We can say then, that battles with time also happen in the future.

Maybe a person says to themselves, "I want to learn how to communicate better. No one seems to get anything I say; people respond to me differently from what I expect. This will always give me trouble." Or, "If 'they' don't do something about fixing the economy, I might end up on the street!"

It is easy to reason that a thinking process of this nature cannot bring anything productive or successful, although some people use it as a motivator to take action and change the things around them. Regrettably, if one is very good at focusing on the possible future demise, without his/her knowledge, the fears accumulate until they could become full blown apprehensions. Still, similar to everything previously discussed, this is also changeable.

NOTE TO THE READER: YOUR BELIEFS AND DECISIONS DETERMINE YOUR BEHAVIOR, WHICH IN TURN CREATE YOUR FUTURE. IF YOU BELIEVE THAT YOU CAN RUN A MILE, YOU WILL. CONVERSELY, IF YOU BELIEVE THAT YOU CANNOT, THEN THAT BELIEF WILL MAKE IT IMPOSSIBLE.

A Taste of Transformation

B eginning with this section, we will proceed to further experimentation with the time line. The reader is advised to precisely follow the given instructions.

Instructions to the Reader

It is useful to give yourself permission to enjoy this process, because lightheartedness is a helpful ingredient. We will still use the same process of active imagination, which means your job is to follow the additional instructions, in your imagination.

Bring to mind the orientation of your time line, and imagine for a moment that you are floating over and above your time line. You can do this however it is comfortable for you, by picturing it, hearing it, or by feeling it. However you imagine it is perfect for you. Once you imagine floating above your time line, make sure you are looking through your own eyes. In other words, you should not see yourself (your body) floating above the time line. If you see yourself floating above the time line, you will not have a positive experience of the process.

Looking through your own eyes, above the time line, you can begin to look down, toward the time line, and notice that your entire time line is within your view. This means that you should imagine yourself floating quite high, so that you can have a full view of the whole length of your time line. As previously discussed, it does not matter if that line is perfectly straight or curved, a circle or an arc, a cork-screw, a tunnel, a pipe filled with memories one next to the other, or just a location in space. If you see something other than a line, adjust these instructions to match your image. If you are seeing, hearing, or feeling it, then you are looking down at the past, present, and future, all stretched out along the time line.

Notice the good feelings that come from looking down on your time line from up above, as if you were up on a mountain observing a beautiful view. It feels good, just for a moment, to be a detached observer of your time line and by extension, of your life. You can see (or hear, or feel) your past, with all its joyous moments, as well as all the moments of trouble and confusion. You see how much you have changed for the better and how much you have progressed and developed. This is probably the most objective, non-threatening and stress-free observer position you can experience.

What does the now-moment look like in your time line? Do you notice how it seems a bit different from the rest of your time line? Some people see a tiny image of themselves during this process; others have just the "sensation" without a clear picture. Fewer people do not see anything at all but intuitively know where it is, and others can feel themselves floating while having a definite feeling of the now-moment. Whatever your imagination, accept it as a message of how you do this unconsciously. This is the way the unconscious mind communicates with the conscious mind.

Spend some time looking at different sections of your time line. Do not go down to visit memories just yet, we will do this together later, for now, remain floating high up above your time line. Notice if you represent the past and future differently. Is one darker than the other? If your future looks bright, might it be an expression of your optimism? If your future looks dark, try to make it brighter. What happens? What are the feelings that you experience while trying to make it brighter?

In general, a valid postulation is that if it is easy to make the future brighter, then you have your time line (and your future) under your control. If it is hard to change, then you are under the control of past events that rule your life – and it is probably a good time to change that.

Once you are done with this part, allow yourself to float back over the past and look for an especially happy memory. Find one that you really like, and float down into that memory. Get in touch with the sights, sounds and feelings of that experience. Make sure you are not seeing yourself in the memory, but that you are in your body at the time, and looking through your own eyes. If you do this well, you will have a huge smile on your face. Pay attention to the colors (if you see pictures), sounds (if you are more auditory), and the feelings in the memory. You might be sensing smells or tastes, as well. If you choose, you can amplify the good feelings from that memory. Perhaps for you, it is as simple as inviting these feelings to come to the forefront of your mind, so that they can fill your senses more completely. Perhaps it is similar to adjusting the controls of a media player in order to increase the intensity, brightness, and other desirable aspects of the experience. Notice how it feels. Spend some time playing with it.

When you are done with this memory, allow yourself to float back above your time line, so high that you can see the whole scope of your life. Spend a moment or two to look around. Did anything change?

When you are ready, float back over the time line to the now-moment, float down into the present, and then back into your body. Take a few minutes to feel yourself fully back in your body.

Depending on how good you naturally are at Time Line Therapy®, your first experience could be quite trance-like, so take a good moment to make sure your awareness is completely back in your body. Do you notice anything different about how it feels to be back? Look around and notice the colors in the room, to complete your full return to the present.

A Time Line Experiment

Now that we have taken note of how the time line looks and feels, during the next process we will focus on creating a happy memory for the future. So far, together we have learned the skills to move above the imaginary time line, to float back above the past, and to enjoy the general view from high-up above. This time, we will take some time to explore the future, and perhaps, to add a little bit of positive influence on the future time line, remembering of course that the future has not happened, yet.

Instructions to the Reader

Before we start, think about an event or a goal that is important to you, an event which you would like to have happen in your future. It is better if that event is for you only rather than for other people. Even if it involves others, this is a goal or an event that you would like for yourself, alone. Think of a possible date for that event, in years, months and even days. Having a particular date in mind helps this process even more.

Once you have a specific and happy event in mind, get in touch with your time line, and with the new skills adopted during the previous process, float high up above the time line. As before, float so high up that you can see your entire time line. This time though, instead of focusing on the past, float out over the future. Go to the desire date of that specific event you have in mind; the event that you would like very much to have happen. Your unconscious mind knows where that event might be located, and it can take you there. Notice, that the event you had considered before you started this exercise, is already in your future time line. This can be surprising for many, but it is just an example of how the unconscious mind takes directions from the conscious mind and executes the requests that were formulated consciously.

Now, make a mental note to remember precisely the position of this event in your time line. Next, take this imagined event out of the time line, as though you were sliding a card out of a deck of playing cards. Look at this future memory and ask yourself, what it is about this event that makes it so desirable? Is there anything in particular? What sensations do you feel while looking at this event's picture? How are the colors of this picture? Are they bright or pale? Are they in focus or less sharp? Is this future memory a still picture or is it a movie? Most important, do you see your body in the picture?

NOTE TO THE READER: WE LOOK AT MEMORIES (AND IMAGINARY FUTURE EVENTS) THROUGH OUR SENSES (SIGHT, SOUND, TASTE, TOUCH), BY OUR FEELINGS, AS WELL AS THROUGH THE WORDS THAT WE SAY TO OURSELVES.

If you imagined receiving an award, for example, perhaps it is desirable to feel the distinction being placed in your hands, or to see the crowd of people smiling at you, or to hear the sound of applause and feel the feeling of accomplishment and excitement. Or, perhaps you put more importance on the fact that you could congratulate yourself and say, "Good work! Well done!"

Keep in mind that, there is a difference between working with past memories, and working with future "goal" memories. In future memories, you should always see your body in the picture, rather than experiencing it through your own eyes like we did in the past. If your body is not in the picture, in other words, if you do not see yourself in the future memory, you literally do not put yourself in that picture, thus leaving yourself out of that goal. And, the result may be that instead of experiencing the achievement yourself, you will observe someone else having that successful event, instead of you. So make certain that you see and hear yourself enjoying the success of that future goal.

NOTE TO THE READER: WHEN WORKING WITH FUTURE MEMORIES, YOU SHOULD ALWAYS SEE YOUR BODY IN THE PICTURE. WE WILL DISCUSS THIS FURTHER IN THE SECTION, "PLANTING SUCCESS IN THE FUTURE"

Make a note of whatever is important to you about that future event, and then amplify it. You can amplify each of your senses. If you imagine expanding your career, see the prominent players (your manager, your boss, or if you are a small business owner, your customers) playfully discussing with you who gets to work with you next. Then, make that image larger, brighter, and more colorful.

How would you make that picture so that it is extremely appealing, and most desirable? What colors are present? What sounds? Is it a movie? Is it a still picture? Try both and notice which one you like the most. Leave the picture with the changes that make you desire it the most. Next, the sounds. Are there any sounds that are important in these future memories? Are there voices or music? Make them louder or softer, and notice which one is the most desirable. After that, you need to amplify your good feelings. If you have done a good job so far, you should be experiencing feelings of excitement, satisfaction, and an overall good, and positive state. Be sure to amplify those felings, and take some time to enjoy them. Change how you observe that future memory so that it is exquisite and extremely desirable.

NOTE TO THE READER: WE ARE NOT CHANGING THE CONTENT OF THAT MEMORY. WE ARE CHANGING THE WAY THAT MEMORY IS STORED, I.E. THE COLORS, THE FOCUS, THE BRIGHTNESS, THE SIZE OF THE PICTURE AND THE CLOSENESS TO YOU AS WELL AS THE PRESENCE OF YOUR BODY IN THE PICTURE. WE ARE ALSO FINE-TUNING THE SOUNDS (MAKING THEM LOUDER OR SOFTER), AND THE GOOD FEELINGS YOU FEEL. THIS IS WHAT MAKES THE DIFFERENCE, NOT THE CONTENT ITSELF. LEAVE THE CONTENT UNCHANGED.

Make whatever changes you need to make to the future memory, **remaining above the time line as you do this work.** This is important. Whether we work on the past or on the future, we always and without exception remain floating above the time line. Now, make that image exceptionally compelling. Emphasize the aspects that you like the most, and which make that goal memory so important to you.

Once all this work is done, place the event back into your time line, remembering the exact place where it belongs. Your unconscious mind will remember the correct place, so just drop it back down into your time line. Notice all the other future memories in your time line between now and that future event, and if you look carefully, you will observe an interesting phenomenon. The insertion of that future memory changes all of the events between it and now. We call this a reevaluation of the time line to support the accomplishment of the new goal you just inserted.

Many things automatically change in order for you to successfully arrive to that future event. Even your now-moment begins to change somewhat, because you – the person who is going to create and experience that future – are a little bit different.

Once done, float back above your time line until you are above the now-moment, and float down into your body, into the present. Take a little time to make sure you are all the way back from the future.

Commentary

While doing this process for the first time, many people are surprised to find that many future memories are already present in their future time line. Our minds are very invested in creating compelling futures for us, but most people never do this with conscious volition. The reality is that, no matter what happened in the past, you really can create your future so that it is richly rewarding, fulfilling, and very happy.

This is the end of our first major time line experience, and the reader was introduced to the powerful force known as "re-evaluation." A single change in one's time line alters many other things so that the time line is in alignment with that change.

Tapping Transformation

More often than not, we are told in personal growth and development books that, in order to create a better future and to stop old patterns productively, we must focus on what we are doing in the now. "Live in the now! Do not think of the future! Forget about the past!" Although there is truth to this statement, few are capable of forgetting the past, or avoiding thoughts about the future. Nevertheless, a focus on the present and future is better than spending years replaying past events through one's mind.

Knowing this, we can move forward to discover how the unconscious mind knows and keeps track of the root cause of your past problems, and how this root cause can be repaired. But first a definition of "root cause" is in order. The root cause is the very first time that a person felt a negative emotion, or formulated a limiting decision or a limiting belief. This is the source of the barrier erected in the unconscious mind, whether one remembers it consciously or not. Eliminating the root cause is one of the most important aspects of working with Time Line Therapy® techniques.

The "Taste of Transformation" exercise, in which we worked with a positive future event in the time line, was just a sliver of what is possible. Repairing a root cause in the past, the source of a current or even future problem, is one of the keys to creating success and changing a negative pattern of behavior.

Some of the readers will understandably be worried that tapping into a root cause can be uncomfortable, or even traumatic, and therefore, they may feel uneasy about the idea of going through the process. Although this is possible, (1) the instances where this happens are very rare, and (2) they happen only for people who have had major trauma, and who can re-experience that trauma just by thinking of it.

Instructions to the Reader

If you are one of those people, or if you are under the supervision of a medical professional, we advise you to refrain from proceeding with the following process.

NOTE TO THE READER: ALTHOUGH TIME LINE THERAPY® TECHNIQUES HAVE BEEN TESTED FOR MORE THAN THIRTY YEARS, AND HAVE BEEN PROVEN TO BE SAFE, IF YOUR CURRENT MENTAL AND PSYCHOLOGICAL HEALTH IS POOR, WE ADVISE YOU TO REFRAIN FROM USING THE FOLLOWING PROCESS. IF YOU WISH TO UNDERSTAND HOW THE PROCESS WORKS AND TO LEARN HOW TO DO THE TECHNIQUES, THEN A BETTER IDEA WOULD BE TO TAKE AN APPROPRIATE TRAINING FROM AN APPROVED TIME LINE THERAPY® INSTITUTE.

At this early point in your exploration of the Time Line Therapy® techniques, a cautionary warning to you is that, for now, you should use these techniques only for your own personal development. There is no justification for attempting to work with more complex problems (1) before receiving adequate training, and (2) if you are under the supervision of a licensed therapist. In these circumstances, you should not attempt to investigate or work with past memories in any form. It is not this author's intention to dampen the reader's enthusiasm with this warning. In fact, the opposite is true. These comments are for one's safe comfort, confidence, and sense of direction.

People who choose to use Time Line Therapy® techniques for their own personal development, often find that they can transform themselves into a person who is better able to use their own capabilities to improve performance at work, and to increase overall satisfaction in life.

The Root Cause

Sorting out the root cause does not require re-association into the event. We are going to use the time line to make the process comfortable. Following the directions of this process, one can find the moment when a limiting decision or a limiting belief about oneself was first made, or the first source of a negative emotion. It is a gentle way of bringing to awareness certain things which were muddled and confused at an unconscious level. The process itself tends to have a calming effect, because, in fact, it allows one to repair, or remove, a barrier that until then was unknown.

In general, Time Line Therapy® techniques do not require one to revisit or relive any past event. In fact, we will spend most of the time above the time line, in a state of dissociation from the original memory.

And in fact, we are at the perfect place to do a process that includes repairing a root cause. Before we begin, let us consider Ty's story.

Ty's Root Cause Elimination

Ty is a creative engineer. Not only is he capable and reliable, but he has inspired ideas. Ty creates things where no one else would have done so. One day, while traveling across one particular bridge in the town where he lived, one creative thought came to his mind. The thought was no less than to build a new modern bridge.

The local politicians and council experts decided it was an impossible accomplishment. The budget was tight, the project was not on the list for the year, and the traffic could be diverted onto an alternative route in case something happened to the old bridge. For the officials, the case was closed – the project had no chance of getting done. It was not practical. It had not been done before, and it would not bring any possible benefits to the economic situation of the town. Nevertheless, the existing bridge was small; the traffic was permanently jammed with trucks, buses, and other heavy vehicles.

Disappointed, Ty pulled back, but could not take his mind off this bridge. Every day, driving to work and back home, he had to cross that bridge. He knew deep in his heart that his bridge plan was possible and that it would bring many benefits to the community. Even so, part of him kept saying that "not all dreams become reality." He had had other creative ideas in the past, even as far back as his childhood. However, most of the time, his father, a very rational man, would caution him to stop dreaming and become a realist.

In school, Ty had also been admonished for being "too creative and too free" with his thoughts, but deep down, he just knew he was right.

One day, he met an old friend over lunch, and the conversation turned to his preferred topic – the bridge. His friend said, "Why don't you talk to other investors, architects, and engineers. Maybe you will get the support you need. Your idea is excellent and surely very useful for everybody in this town." "I tried many times," said Ty, and "I have also failed many times. I always heard criticism". And I am tired of hearing "I told you so," and "You're a fool chasing wild visions. Why don't you just settle down and be an ordinary person like us the rest of us." On one hand, I would like to make this project work but on the other, why bother even trying? Just to get disappointed again?"

Ty continued the conversation by complaining that every time he had tried in the past, he was dismissed and called a dreamer. He did not see the point in going through such an intense experience again. Aside from that, he was also worried that pursuing his dreams would affect him financially, or hurt his personal or family life. Most importantly, he feared what would happen if he actually found success.

The friend then asked him when he decided that all of his attempts would end up in failure. And as it often happens, Ty couldn't remember anything consciously, although he tried. But as he pondered over the possible memory, an answer popped into his head. "I don't know what to make of this," he said, "but I have a feeling that it was when I was one year old ... but then, I don't remember anything from that time. Is this right?"

"Trust your intuition," his friend said, "even if you don't know where the answer came from, because it came from within you. Your unconscious mind is at work, and it is always right."

"This is too bizarre," said Ty. "I know I didn't think of this consciously. I didn't hear a little voice inside my head, but I had this intuition that it was at age one. I just felt like saying age one."

And so, Ty discovered to his amazement that the root cause of his dis-belief that he could actually go on with his creative ideas happened very early in life when he was a very young child. Then, his friend guided him further through the Time Line Therapy® process, where Ty understood and made rational the purpose for which he had originally made that decision. In fact, Ty realized that the belief was not even his alone, but borrowed from his father. He also discovered how, some other opportunities, where he could have had a different experience, were missed because of the decision that he had made a long time ago. In several instances, if he pursued his ideas just a little more, he could have made them happen. The old belief though, made him give up too early, never bringing his brilliant ideas to fulfillment. He preserved his new understandings and rationalizations about the root cause situation, and let go of the whole need to have that pattern happen again.

After that, Ty phoned some important people in his town and asked for appointments. He developed a concise plan of how to get investments and use the funds most effectively to accomplish this project. He also had a clear account of what the benefits to the community would be, and of how his plan could provide the community with a significant return on its investment. Ty used compressed data and numbers to persuade the community leaders and investors that the bridge not only could be, but had to be built. Soon after that, with great excitement and inspiration, Ty began building his dream bridge.

The obstacles we face in our everyday lives usually stem from events in the past – events that we may not even remember consciously. Ty's example shows us that repetitive patterns come from somewhere in the past, but that these patterns disappear when we learn the greater purpose for which they were originally created. When we rationalize their meaning, it becomes easy to disconnect the patterns from our memories and to proceed anew, free of past barriers. Dreams that seem impossible, situations that we cannot seem to conquer, and patterns that we keep repeating, can be solved successfully with desire, determination, and persistence, no matter the odds.

Finding the Root Cause

Before one can let go of an old negative emotion, a limiting decision, or a limiting belief, one needs to discover where the root cause for that particular emotion, decision, or belief is located. Each one will have a different root cause.

People who do gardening know that if one wants to get rid of weeds, the wrong thing to do is to mow them over or cut them off at top soil level. Even worse is to try and pull off the leaves. The net result will be counterproductive. The weeds will simply grow again, and in many cases, even stronger and sturdier than before. The only way to truly get rid of a weed is to pull it all out of the ground, roots et al, all at once.

Similarly, in order to let go of a negative emotion, a limiting decision, or a limiting belief that bothers us, we need to find its very roots.

Instructions to the Reader

To find the root cause for a negative emotion, a limiting

decision, or a limiting belief, ask yourself the following question: "What was the first event, the very first time this happened in my life?" An age will pop into your head very quickly. Make sure that you avoid trying to think consciously of an event. Remember that your conscious mind is not responsible for storing and organizing your memories, it is your unconscious mind that does this, so trust the first thing that comes into your mind. All you need is a number which evidently represents your age at the time. Ideally, the number will be somewhere between the time of your birth and age seven, but whatever it is, take the first number that comes to mind. Make a note of it; you will use it later.

> NOTE TO THE READER: DO NOT TRY TO FIND THE MEMORY BY CONSCIOUSLY STRIVING TO REMEMBER THE CONTENT OR THE STORY OF THAT EVENT. THIS IS A USUAL TENDENCY FOR BEGINNERS IN TIME LINE THERAPY®. IN TIME LINE THERAPY® WE ARE NOT CONCERNED WITH THE CONTENT OF THE MEMORY. WE ARE NOT RECOVERING MATERIAL, AND THE MEMORY ITSELF MAKES NO DIFFERENCE. TIME LINE THERAPY® IS A STRUCTURAL PROCESS THAT SIMPLY CHANGES THE WAY THE MEMORY IS STORED AT THE UNCONSCIOUS LEVEL. THEREFORE, ALL YOU NEED IS A NUMBER, WHICH REPRESENTS THE AGE YOU WERE AT THE TIME.

Your reassurance that you found the real root cause, rather than a later event, is when the number comes from early in your life, before the age of seven. Most of our negative emotions, and even limiting decisions and limiting beliefs stem from that period. We are too young to rationalize things consciously, and we react with an irrational, childlike, and unconscious emotional response that leads to unhelpful decisions, behaviors, and attitudes. Sometimes we just borrow limiting decisions and limiting beliefs from our parents, close relatives, or childhood friends. Even watching a movie could have a similar effect on young minds. Nevertheless, such a decision, belief, or negative emotion, if it is still bothersome to us on a regular basis, will have the same unconscious reaction, in spite of our better judgment.

It is possible that, at that age, we were too young to even remember the memory itself. It is also possible that the event itself was not memorable at all. Not all sources of negative emotions, limiting decisions and limiting beliefs are rooted in major events. To put it simply, not all root causes are significant. Some are extremely basic, day-to-day, and innocent occurrences, which, consciously, do not warrant a second look. However, unconsciously they made a big impression.

It is important to find the root cause, which is to say, the very first time when, compared to what you are experiencing now, something similar ever happened. It may be easy to overlook the root cause at first, because (1) either you have learned to ignore it or (2) deny its importance, or (3) it was not important to begin with. After all, you had to get on with your life.

Furthermore, your unconscious mind may try to help you by keeping the root cause tucked neatly away. It is always trying to smooth your path and take away distractions until it gets permission to bring up the root cause for resolution. It usually only does this when you have connected with your unconscious mind in a way that tells it to trust the process. These trustworthy conditions are essential when doing Time Line Therapy®.

In the upcoming section, you will hear the word "re-evaluate." As in the previous chapter, this means that events throughout the time line are adjusting to the change so that the entire time line is harmonious. It is similar to science fiction stories where everyone's memories fit into a new universe they have never visited. Except that here, your mind will learn to change the meaning of your memories. The change in the encoding of your memories makes them different and more efficient in your time line, although the content of your memories remains unchanged.

NOTE TO THE READER: IN TIME LINE THERAPY® WE DO NOT CHANGE THE CONTENT OF THE MEMORIES, RATHER, YOU CHANGE THE MEANING OF THE MEMORIES BY PRESERVING THE LEARNINGS OF THE ROOT CAUSE EVENT. IN THIS WAY, WE CAN LET GO OF OLD NEGATIVE EMOTIONS, LIMITING DECISIONS, AND LIMITING BELIEFS.

Making changes in the meaning associated with the event and letting go of negative emotions from the past, will not make you believe wrong things, but it will reconnect you with inner resources that will make you stronger and more resourceful.

From Fear to Freedom

In the next section we will explain the process of letting go of fear using Time Line Therapy®. Before we do that, there are some important things to remember. Some of us overreact to signals of danger, and some of us underreact, but we all have instincts and intuitions that produce fear and keep us alive. So, fear, as an emotion, is necessary. Sometimes the fear is founded, but more often than not, it is not even real – it is an apparent or alleged danger.

NOTE TO THE READER: THIS TECHNIQUE WILL NOT TAKE AWAY YOUR ABILITY TO FEEL FEAR IN THE PRESENT OR IN THE FUTURE IF A SITUATION WARRANTS IT. IF ANYTHING, IT CAN SHARPEN YOUR INSTINCTUAL REACTION. UNDER- AND OVER-REACTORS DEAL WITH THEIR INSTINCTS AND INTUITIONS MORE EFFICIENTLY WHEN STORED FEAR IS RELEASED FROM PAST MEMORIES.

As we have seen in the section "Why Fear Paralyzes You," avoiding anger and fear does not solve the problem. Whenever, even if unwillingly, we encounter situations where we do get angry or fearful, swallowing the emotions and pretending they are not there will not make us feel better. We do not want to have these events victimize us forever.

For the next process, you can think of any fears that are a nuisance to you, such as fear of a social situation or some challenge you have been postponing. If you cannot readily think of one, look back to the questionnaire you completed at the beginning of this book. You can take any fear you checked there and work on it to let it go. Even self-doubt is something to work on, as it creates fear of future performance. Whichever you choose to work on, you will feel much better when you are done!

Let us say, for example, that in your past you had a relationship breakup. Although that relationship is long gone, you may now feel unfounded fear and anxiety in present relationships. In turn, these fears could lead to sabotage (of self, relationships, or both) as you try to protect yourself from further heartache. If those emotions are present, you will not be able to thoroughly enjoy new relationships. Releasing fear can restore balance and clarity, freeing you from fear-based limitations that no longer serve you.

Of course, many of our limiting fears got their start from a real need. Consider the very common fear of success. Many people sabotage their careers and businesses because of unnecessary fears that are holding them back. If you think back, you can probably remember at least one time when you did not engage in an activity that would have boosted your success.

To give you a few familiar examples, we could mention the fear of networking, reaching out to an important person, raising your rates in your own business, taking on a new challenge, talking to your boss, renegotiating a deal, dating someone, telling somebody off, and the list could go on.

Although all of these examples could fit under the big umbrella of fear of success, it is recommendable that you work on them one by one.

Fear Away, Welcome Determination

Instructions to the Reader

Choose a fear that you would like to work on, such as one from the test, and make sure it is only one example of fear or one statement.

NOTE TO THE READER: WORK ON ONE STATEMENT AT A TIME.

Frist, write down the fear you want to let go of. It is important to write it down explicitly. Just holding it in your mind is not sufficient. As an example, we will take "I am afraid of failing."

Next, ask yourself, "What was the first event, when was the very first time this happened in my life?" For example, you would say, "When was the first time I failed at something?"

Instruct your unconscious mind to give you only an age, not the content of the memory. What happened then is not important for our process. This could be counterintuitive, because in general, we are all trying to remember the content of a memory thinking that if we remember it correctly, we will find out why it happened. However, for Time Line Therapy®, this is not important. All you want is an age.

Taking our example, "I am afraid of failing" it would be counterproductive to try and remember the first memory consciously. "Well, I remember my school teacher wanted me to be the captain of the football team, but I was afraid that I would fail. But I also remember when my first boss offered me a project and I failed to complete it successfully." This is incorrect, because this process involves a conscious analysis, and your target here is to have your unconscious mind to give you an age only.

If age two, or five, or seven comes to mind, even if you do not remember consciously what happened then, you are doing the process correctly.

Now, close your eyes and imagine you are floating up above your imaginary time line. Ask your unconscious mind to float you high up above your time line, and then back over your past to the time when this happened for the very first time. You may see a flash of light, a color, or a dark or bright spot in your time line. You may notice a sound, a feeling, or an inner "knowing" indicating where the event is. Then float out well before the event occurred. This time you are supposed to be well before the event has happened, and also you must turn so that you're looking toward now, and the event is in front of you, down in the time line.

NOTE TO THE READER: REMAIN FLOATING HIGH UP ABOVE THE TIME LINE. DO NOT ATTEMPT TO GO DOWN IN THE EVENT. THE PURPOSE OF THIS EXERCISE IS NOT TO REVISIT THE EVENT, BUT TO GET THE MEANING AND LEARNINGS FROM IT. LEARNING FROM THE EVENT IS THE KEY TO YOUR SUCCESS.

An old adage says that "all things in life happen for a reason." The reason is that even negative events, once we comprehend their meaning and once we integrate the learnings, could help us grow and learn something important. From these events, we become wiser, more responsible, and more mature.

Therefore, remaining above the time line, and before the event, ask yourself the following question: "What learnings are there to learn here, learnings which will allow the fear to totally and completely disappear? What was the purpose of this event in my life? What deeper meaning did I not notice before? What was there for me to understand?"

As you ponder on learnings and meanings, make sure what comes to your mind is for you and you alone, not for others. These are your learnings and it may not seem obvious that you cannot learn things for other people. Moreover, those learnings must be of a positive nature. This is the process by which they can be used for your future, as empowering and positive resources. Once you get the learnings, you will notice that the fear disappears. The only purpose for it remaining in your time line was to serve you as a teacher. Once you learn what there is to learn, the teacher goes away.

From our example of "I am afraid of failing," your newfound understanding and learning could be that if you never try something, you will never know if you could be successful. Maybe you will realize that it is all right to fail from time to time. Failure does not mean that you are a bad person; it just gives you something to learn from. The most successful people in the world became successful because they were not afraid to fail; they tried again and again until they reached the pinnacle of success. Perhaps another learning could be related to more effectively observing the situations in which you find yourself, and to prepare well in advance for new challenges.

Maybe you will see that failure at that time has made you better at some things, or that it helped you build character. Perhaps you will find that if you had never failed, you could think you are above everyone else. Look for the lessons and deeper meanings that will allow you to let go of the fear.

Once you find those learnings, the fear disappears from the

time line. Before you started this exercise, you knew the fear was there, but after this part of the process, you may not know where it went. You cannot see it, and you cannot feel it anymore. And this is precisely how you will know that it is not there.

If the fear has disappeared, you can be reassured that it has been replaced by the lessons and deeper meanings, which, of course, your unconscious mind has incorporated for the future.

As soon as the fear has disappeared, still floating above the time line, come back towards the now-moment, while you let go of all the fear from your time line. There were other instances in your time line, whenever you experienced the same type of fear. Make sure you let it all go. Stop above each one of the additional events in your timeline where there was more fear, remaining safely above the time line all the time, get more learnings and let go of all the additional fear by preserving extra learnings, if necessary. For some people there are extra learnings, for others the whole fear disappears at once. As you do this process, notice how the time line cleans itself of all the old fear. When you arrive above the now-moment, float down into your body, and come back fully in the present. Open your eyes, stretch a little bit, and "ground" yourself in the present by noticing the colors in your environment.

If you want to remember the learnings, now is the time to write them down.

Guilt Eraser

Instructions to the Reader

Now we will go together through the process of releasing guilt. Think of a past event that you feel guilty about. If nothing comes to mind, pick something that has brought you shame. If you look through your past regrets, something that triggers shame should come up.

Float above your time line, and float back well before the guilt-filled or shameful event occurred.

IMPORTANT: DO NOT ATTEMPT TO GO DOWN IN THE EVENT. REMAIN FLOATING ABOVE THE TIME LINE. THE PURPOSE IS NOT TO REVISIT THE EVENT, BUT TO GET THE MEANING AND THE LEARNINGS FROM IT.

Ask yourself, "What is there to learn from this event in my life?" What deeper meaning did you not notice before? What new understandings can you get from the event? As you answer these questions, and as you find the learnings and deeper meanings of the event, the guilt disappears. Follow the same process of acquiring the learnings as for fear. Make sure you restructure the meaning of the event in your mind, so you get the most positive and empowering resources for the future.

These learnings should be only for you, not for others. Examples of possible positive learnings could be something of this nature "I was young and I did not know what I was doing. Now, I am older and I see that my behavior was not useful and it gave me and others a lot of trouble." Or, "I was doing the best I could with the resources I had available to me at that time. I can let it go now since I have learned so much (be specific here with what you have learned) since then." Or it might say something like this, "I can let go of this guilt now, this guilt has no need to be here any longer. It has served its purpose because (insert here the new learnings)."

If you do a good job, and you acquire the necessary learnings, you will not only ensure that the guilt disappears, but also that you will not make the same mistake again. At this point, most everyone finds that the disturbing feeling of guilt has been destroyed, it just sort of popped and is now gone.

When that happens, ask yourself, "Now, where is the guilt? Is it there, or has it disappeared, now?"

If the guilt did not disappear, it is because you are not willing to forgive yourself for past mistakes. Just know that holding onto that guilt will not make you a better person, but, preserving the learnings arising from the event will. Guilt does not stop you from repeating mistakes or old behaviors, and it is not by feeling guilt that you apologize. Forgiving yourself is possible when you learn what you needed to learn, though. By preserving the learnings, you will gain more resourceful behaviors.

As soon as the guilt has disappeared, begin your journey back, remaining safely floating above the time line, and moving toward the now-moment. As you do, let go of all the guilt from other memories in the time line. Stop above each one, remaining safely above the time line, get more learnings if necessary, and let go of all the additional guilt by preserving all the additional learnings.

When you are done, float all the way back to the now-moment, and float back down into your body in the present. Open your eyes, stretch a little bit, and "ground" yourself in the present by noticing the colors in your environment.

If you have been successful so far and feel different about your old guilt, then you have done the process correctly. Why not let go of all the other negative emotions using the same process? You could look over the list of negative emotions that you checked while completing the questionnaire. If there are others, you could eliminate them one by one using the same process.

Planting Success in The Future

Success, fulfillment, accomplishment and high performance do not happen by magic, although it could feel like something miraculous. This chapter demonstrates how to use the future time line and metaphorically, how to become the creator of one's future.

If the reader aspires to create a future which consists of desired events, a compelling and exciting future instead of the proverbial "whatever," there are some things that could be done. There are some key components we could use, all related to the future time line, which once put in place, can influence our motivation and drive, which in turn will make that future possible.

The "Taste of Transformation" section presents the basic version of this process. In the following section, we will examine other details about how to turn that process into a powerful method for creating the future one desires.

Firstly, we will present the requirements for creating a "SMART Goal," which is incredibly helpful in all aspects of life that require planning. Once we learn how to create and recognize a SMART Goal, the reader will be able to see the gaps in any plan.

Then, we will touch a little on the magic of temporal (i.e. time related) language to alter one's experience of time. Although we will barely touch this subject, and at a very basic level, it could be surprising to find out that the words and their description of time could assist one in creating positive mental imagery. A mind filled with positive imageries (and the reader will remember that our thoughts contain images, sounds, and feelings) will direct the behaviors far more efficiently than a mind focused on negativity.

A considerable part of how we experience our past negative emotions has to do with our thoughts, and these are bound in time. The language of time combines the power of thought patterns and time perception to allow these old emotions to disappear. This understanding enables the reader to produce personal change in rapid and surprising ways, especially when combined with other strategies from the following chapters.

Finally, we will discuss the importance of correct focusing, desire, and action.

NOTE TO THE READER: THESE ARE NOT METHODS FOR CREATING PLEASANT FANTASIES, NOR ARE THEY TO HELP THE READER TO RESOLVE MEDICAL PROBLEMS. IT IS A MEANS OF CREATING COMPELLING GOALS THAT ALIGN ONE'S MIND AND RESOURCES TOWARD ACHIEVABLE, MEANINGFUL OUTCOMES.

How Sofia and Her Team Created a Future of Success

One of the best examples of future-creation legends is Sofia. She worked in a corporation on a low managerial level. Although accomplished and talented, she felt that good luck had eluded her career, and she was determined to change that.

As in all corporations, and depending on the situation, the manager's results are measured by the success of the whole team. Sofia and her sales team were part of a mortgage company, and their performance was comparatively efficient, but they never succeeded in reaching the highpoint of performance she desired. Sofia had reached a plateau of "all right," but no matter how hard she and her team worked, they did not seem proficient enough to move forward and further the development of her department.

Motivated to create more income for the business, and to better performance her own, Sofia tried many motivational methods. Once acquainted with Time Line Therapy® techniques, it did not take long for her to realize that she and her team had many fears and limiting decisions about their ability to create new business. New clients seemed reluctant to engage, and she discovered, to her surprise, that a feeling of not being good enough started edging its way into her mind. Notwithstanding her past excellent accomplishments, Sofia did not feel capable enough to sell or serve people effectively in a changing economic environment.

In effect, Sofia discovered a major limitation when negotiating deals involving amounts greater than $300,000. She also noticed a belief that nobody would be willing to invest now, and that because she "came from the wrong side of the tracks," she would not be able to successfully engage new prospects. On her side, Sofia had integrity, and she always wanted to make deals that suited the customer as well as the corporation she worked for; in other words, she was always concerned with creating a win for both parties involved.

With help from the "Fear Away, Welcome Determination" process, and from letting go of some significant limitations, she achieved a major shift in perspective. She learned the difference between achievable and unachievable goals, and increased her business volume ten-fold times as a result. Her team welcomed the shift, and her belief in her own abilities skyrocketed. She now plans to teach this herself for the new generation of mortgage lenders.

There seems to be some truth to the old adage that says, "Whether you believe you can do something, or not, you are right."

S.M.A.R.T. Goals

Most people have set goals for themselves at one time or another. Whether they did this process consciously and with volition, or only thought about the things they wanted to achieve, most of us are familiar with the notion of setting goals for the future. If the reader is like most people, some of his/her past goals have happened the way s/he envisioned them, and others failed to materialize. In this process, we will attempt to describe what the key differences are between the two.

In relation to future goals, S.M.A.R.T. is not a new acronym. Nevertheless, it is very useful as it provides the initials that will help the reader to formulate his/her goals:

- Specific, Simple, and Stated positively
- Measurable and Meaningful
- As if Now, (In Present Tense) and Achievable
- Realistic and Responsible
- Timed and Toward what you want

1. Specific, Simple, and Stated positively

In order to think of a goal in a way that increases the chances for success, it is better to state the goal in positive terms. Simplicity is another determinant factor that influences the potential for the goal to take place in the way one desires. Long, convoluted goals with out-clauses will not work as well as goals that are stated simply and directly. Many times, in their desire not to miss out, people state goals which include other secondary objectives. "If goal A does not happen, then I will go after goal B and if that does not succeed I will then proceed to goal C." This is not a formula for success. Formulate one clear goal, simply stated, and follow through without out-clauses.

Nevertheless, to formulate a clear, simple, and specific goal, first, one needs to know **specifically** what is desired. The reader would be surprised to find out how many people do not have any notion about the specificity of what they want. For these individuals, the description of what they want would be a very vague idea of "more money," "more happiness," and a "better life." All these three examples are (1) not specific and (2) not precisely defined. At the risk of sounding redundant, we must mention that "more money" is not specific. One penny extra in the pocket is "more money." Therefore, for the SMART goals to work most efficiently, numbers and percentages work the best; and comparatives such as "more" or "better" do not produce the anticipated results.

Instructions to the Reader

Therefore, when thinking of the SMART conditions, specificity works and abstractions are undesirable. An easy process for finding out specifically what is desirable, is to begin by asking yourself the question, what it is that you do not want anymore? Once you have that answer, then ask yourself, "What do I want instead?" This may take some practice if you are not habitually coherent or if you are unclear about what you want.

Although the topic of negative thinking was addressed in previous chapters, the importance of this issue cannot be overstated. Focusing exclusively on what could go wrong can act as an energy drain. The principle applied by all intelligent and successful business people is to first consider what could go wrong, then take preventive measures, and then focus on the positive outcome to the exclusion of everything else. This principle can be applied with the same success in all goals, business, career, or otherwise.

This could be particularly important if one has failed in achieving one's objectives in the past. The disappointment of failing can keep people from trying again. Unfortunately, many people are too concerned with not getting hurt (i.e. avoiding what they don't want) to go after what they truly do want. Unwanted thoughts, particularly unconscious ones, mix with the conscious wants and desires, and until they are attended to, made conscious, and then changed, they will inhibit progress.

Let us discuss a specific example. Sometimes we have an exceedingly stressful day. This can happen more often than not. At the end of the said long day, all we want to do is to put it all away and find refuge in a good night's sleep. But when bedtime comes, thoughts of the day still roll around in one's mind. Those thoughts come from the day's unfinished business, as well as the negative emotions or limiting decisions and beliefs experienced throughout the day. A particularly stressful day, (note the word **stressful**) implies an emotionally filled day, even if the emotions are experienced only at the unconscious level. A day like this could leave us feeling tired, drained, and overwhelmed by the day's problems. Although a good night's sleep is helpful, it does not put thoughts to rest when they come from unresolved emotions. Combine that with future fears, worries, and uncertainties about how to proceed, and one has the perfect recipe for the beginning of a new negative thought pattern. Left unchecked, this new pattern has the potential to attach itself to old and similar situations, and it will continue to worsen if left alone.

By gaining control of one's emotional response to daily experiences, one dramatically improves the quality of one's life as well as the potential to solve the current problems with a much cleaner mental environment.

The reader is advised to remember that our thoughts are the blueprints for our actions and behaviors, and so they become skeletal frameworks for the future. Our thoughts and behaviors are influenced and depend on how we view things. The lessons and re-evaluations stimulated by Time Line Therapy® processes have the potential of changing how we see our life experiences.

Many of us are not aware of how much negativity is within our thoughts and attitudes. No matter our age, gender, or socio-economic background, if we wish to improve the conditions of our future, we must cut out negative thought patterns to provide different instructions to our time line, therefore changing it for the better. By stripping away old, nonessential, and counterproductive blueprints, we increase our efficiency and ability to focus on what we truly want, which is imperative to fulfillment, greater productivity, and success.

Admittedly, it takes courage and humbleness to admit that a cherished belief system may not be working as well as we thought. Once we realize that without certain beliefs we used to consider "true," we could have attained better results, we get an entirely different perspective. However, if we choose to continue to blame the outside environment alone for our misfortunes, we will be unable to change things to our satisfaction.

"I could have been a success if it weren't for _____," does not work as good as, "I could have avoided _____, but at the time it was the only thing I thought I could do, and now I have more resources to proceed."

In fact, when we shift our focus we can begin to notice different things. Everything we own, material or otherwise, and everything we have achieved, is a product of our positive thoughts. Similarly, everything we do not own or have failed to achieve, is a product of our negative thoughts. Naturally, this is not a popular view of life. It has the potential to make one feel bad at the realization that life could have been different, if only one would have thought and behaved in a different way. Nevertheless, that would be again a negative focus, filled with regret, guilt, shame, and other possible negative emotions.

Another significant consideration is to pay attention to our own mental games. One of our students made the following remark. "I cannot control what I think. Thoughts seem to come from nowhere and I cannot put them away no matter how hard I try." He further stated that this is just the way he feels and there is not much he could do about it."

The reality is that even in such a situation there is something one can do, all the while remembering that one's thoughts are based on beliefs and decisions mixed with emotions from the past. As we have seen, Time Line Therapy® techniques can change that. Knowing specifically what we want is of utmost importance.

Instructions to the Reader

Here are a few examples of changing one's thinking from what one does not want anymore, into what one could want instead. If you do not wish to be stuck in a small town, does that mean you want to live in the big city? If not, where would you like to live? If you are tired of the hustle and bustle of city life, does that mean you want to be a pig farmer? If you are sick of being treated poorly in your relationship, does that mean that you want to be alone? If you do not wish to be poor, does that mean that you want to be a billionaire? If you want to accumulate more wealth, do you think wealthy people do things out of integrity? If you do, and you associate money with lack of integrity, unconsciously you may not be motivated to make money because you do not want to do anything out of integrity. What other beliefs are counterproductive to your desire to be prosperous?

This introspection helps your unconscious mind to understand the conscious mind's instructions without inconsistencies. Paradoxically, this process could improve your clarity of mind and thinking process, and, therefore, increase your persuasion and leadership skills. In relation to you, others want to know where you stand, and they will respect your ability to state what you want when you do so in positive terms.

Write down your goal and read it carefully. If necessary, rewrite it several times and reword it until it is stated in specific, simple, and positive words. Start with a simple statement of your goal. Use just a few words, and make them short words. If you are not sure how to do that, say or write everything that is on your mind about the goal. Then do it again, eliminating whatever you can without really compromising the essence of the goal. Keep doing this until you have reduced it to something that resembles an advertising slogan.

One of the benefits of simplicity is that it forces you to get to the essence of your goal. Not only does this align you within, i.e. conscious mind and unconscious mind together, but it gives you a reference point from where to begin your thinking process. This is similar to the "talking points" that politicians use; they may say all sorts of things, but they are usually improvising from a very short list of talking points, especially when in the media spotlight.

2. Measurable and Meaningful

Setting measurable goals works well because it gives one a quantifying way to evaluate where one is in relation to where one wants to be. It also allows one to recognize if one has arrived at the desired goals, or even the percentage to which one were successful.

Instructions to the Reader

Pegging down your goal with specific details, such as figures and dates, benefits you in a number of ways. Did you say you want to make more money? How much money and by when? Did you say you want a better relationship? What exactly does "better" mean? Did you say you wish to lose weight? What is your ideal weight and by when do you want to achieve that target? If your goal has to do with improving your business' bottom line, well then, ask yourself "By how much and by when?" Note: there is no relationship between gross sales and net income. Therefore, when you set goals for business growth, always use the word "net" in your goal.

Because the unconscious mind works on the principle of "least effort," you need to make sure your unconscious mind has the right details. You do not want to unconsciously think, "I made a dollar today, this is more money!" Obviously, this is an exaggerated example; however, we hope you get the idea. It is not specific enough to say that you want to make $5,000 more per month. The word "more" makes it unclear, because we do not know to what the comparison is made. More than what? Than nothing? Than what you currently make? At the unconscious level, the comparison does not make sense, although it may be logical to the reasoning of the conscious mind. Therefore, a goal of this nature works best if you specify the actual amount that you want to make per month.

Perhaps one of the most important elements of the "Measurable" part of your SMART conditions is to track your progress and make adjustments as you go. This is crucial to creating a measurable goal. If you miss a deadline or a particular detail specified in your goal, you can then review your plan, learn from the process, and make adjustments to your methods.

If you take some time to work through these details, they will automatically reinforce your plan in your future time line. Dates and durations tell you when to insert events in your time line, and this network of goals and plans will also act as motivators, and enhancers for your drive, confidence, and congruence.

The word "Meaningful," in relation to goals, refers to the goal's **meaningfulness and relevance to you specifically.** It is critical to realize that you cannot set goals for other people. "I want my partner to act in X manner" is not a goal for you, but for your partner. You can share the process with your children, colleagues at work, or partner, and let them set goals for themselves. Furthermore, this method can be utilized to decide on common goals for a team, and then, each individual will insert the goal in his/her future time line. But trying to set goals for others will end up in frustration and disappointment; it will not work.

NOTE TO THE READER: THE READER WILL BE ADVISED TO REMEMBER THAT THE PROCESS OF TIME LINE THERAPY® AND THE WAY WE UTILIZE THE TIME LINE FOR CREATING A FULFILLING AND COMPELLING FUTURE, IS NOT "MAGIC," BUT A VERY CLEARLY DEFINED, LOGICAL SERIES OF STEPS, WHICH, IF FOLLOWED CORRECTLY, CAN CHANGE OUR BEHAVIORS AND, THEREFORE, OUR RESULTS.

By the same token, do not chase your parents' or other people's goals as though they were for you. Make sure that what you say is really what you desire. If you are incongruent or incoherent and act to please others, your results will not be as good, or they may fail to materialize entirely. To put it simply, make sure that every goal springs from your true self and generates genuine passion in your heart.

When a part of you, either consciously or unconsciously, feels that your goal will not support an aspect of your current values or belief structure, the result is a certain incongruence-type feeling. It could feel like a little glitch. This glitch could be an unconscious (or even conscious) belief or decision you made in the past that is opposed to your conscious wishes or desires. If you can discover it, it is recommendable to let go of that belief or decision with Time Line Therapy® techniques; otherwise, it will work against your goal. As you engineer out the details of the goal, keep an eye out for these aspects that you may need to adjust.

Let us take a simple example. If you hesitate to take steps that will make your career take off, you need to find out specifically what belief or decision is creating that resistance. Often times, people get so excited about future plans, or about the development of a new business outcome, that they forget to pay attention to any signs warning of incongruence.

Therefore, as you read the goal you are working on, pay attention to your thinking and feeling as you read it. Do you have a feeling of uneasiness? Do you have doubts? Do you think, "It would be nice, but I do not believe that I will actually get it"?

All of these examples and more are possible. As you contemplate your goal's specificity, measurable-ness, and meaningfulness, if you pay attention to the internal response that you experience, you could come across the unconscious mind trying to tell you that maybe you forgot something. If you are starting a new business, did you make time in your plan to learn the essential skills? Do you have at least basic notions of marketing and advertising? Are you good at making sales? Did you thoroughly analyze the business, or did you rely on hype from those who benefit from your participation in the business? Setting goals in one's future time line is not a replacement for thorough and critical thinking. It works in collaboration with said matters and it increases the chances for it to happen.

3. Know the starting point
(As if Now, In Present Tense, and Achievable)

The most effective way of thinking about future goals is to begin by explicitly understanding the situation as it is now, and this refers to As if now, (in the present) and Achievable.

Instructions to the Reader

The more specificity you have about the situation as it is now, the better your assessment and comparison between the starting point and the fulfillment of the goal. This helps evaluate your progress as time goes by. If your goal is set up for a year, at six months into the year you should be half way toward your goal. If you are not, naturally, there are some changes to be made (1) to the way you act and do things in regard to your goal, (2) in your motivation and determination to achieve what you have set up for a goal, and (3) maybe a change in your beliefs, future worries, and inability to take action. Your starting point also helps you assess your needs and strengths in order to ensure that your plan is truly relevant and complete.

If you want to move to a city with better career options, then you need to recognize your requirements as well as your current assets. Do you have the finances necessary for moving and establishing yourself? If not, what ways could you conceive of making this possible? Do you have good contacts for getting a good job position in a new location? If not, what do you need to do in that respect? Are you specific about what kind of job you are thinking of? If you are not, then, it is time to also spend some time considering this subject. If yes, do you have the necessary social skills to take full advantage of those contacts? These questions and others of a similar nature can help you clarify your starting point. If your answer is "no" to any of these questions, you may need to learn some new skills, or to adopt new strategies.

Subsequently, keep in mind how you state your goal to adjust for the time issue. Goals that are stated in the future tense tend to slide further away in the time line, as the unconscious mind receives the instructions to think of this for the future. At the unconscious level, that translates as a permanent future. By stating the goal as if it were true now, in the present tense, you help your unconscious mind "get" the real meaning of the goal. Your unconscious mind focuses a lot on what seems real in the present, so stating goals as if they were true will help your internal alignment. If you state it as if it is happening now, it is also easier to see any flaws or preparations you might have missed. It is a bit like looking at plans before building a house, and then looking at a drawing of the house in its context. The drawing or the graphic image will give you a completely different perception because it is much closer to reality than the plans.

NOTE FOR THE READER: GOALS STATED "AS IF NOW" HAVE A

GREATER CHANCE OF BEING ACCOMPLISHED COMPARED TO GOALS STATED IN FUTURE TENSE. IF YOU SET A GOAL FOR WEIGHT, THEN YOU CAN USE THE FOLLOWING LITTLE FORMULA: "IT IS NOW _____ (INSERT HERE THE DATE BY WHICH YOU WANT TO ACCOMPLISH YOUR GOAL) AND I NOW WEIGH X"

The next thing to keep in mind is whether the goals you want to insert in your future time line are achievable by you. There are no miracles outside of those you create. If your goal is financial, and you (1) do not expect an inheritance, or (2) do not have investments with a significant return, it is hard to conceive that you could become a millionaire overnight. If your goal is about getting into a good physical shape, keep in mind whether you are also willing to work out and change a current diet that may not be supporting your goals. The only judge of whether a goal is achievable or not is you. These criteria are "As if now" and "Achievable."

Mason's Time Line Therapy® Goal Achievement

Mason's law career was full of anguish, and he fretted over how to get out of it. Although he was a knowledgeable and experienced lawyer, he felt conflicted about his job. Every day he would go to work thinking, "Oh no! Not again!" until the thought of quitting his job became apparent. There was a setback, though.

He was not really qualified to do anything other than practice law. His skills, although extremely useful and financially rewarding, were in a niche, but he was bored and wanted a change. He had spent years in law school and was a specialist in his field. The recurring questions in his mind were, "Do I want to give up my career entirely? Is there some way to combine my knowledge with other, equally as important interests? If I abandon my career, what else can I do? How much money will I earn? How do I find a new career that fulfills me?"

When one starts a new career, or follows a particular path for some time, it is not easy to think that something broader could be available. Overall, we have invested years of effort and work into a career which although boring, is fulfilling a number of needs. We go to medical school to become a doctor or a veterinarian. We complete an apprenticeship to become IT technicians. We specialize in dentistry to become a dentist, and so it makes sense that if one goes to law school, one wants to be a lawyer.

Mason was running in circles wanting to change something but felt that he did not have many options and, therefore, could not change anything. He could not imagine himself doing anything else. His law career paid the bills, and ensured for a comfortable lifestyle and consequently he could not fathom making more money and earning better benefits by doing anything else. Yet, Mason was not happy. He had very little personal satisfaction from his job.

Some of his family members were encouraging him in a very nice "New Age" fashion. "Just take a leap into the unknown. Just do it and the universe will support you! Resign your position, and then you will see how quickly new opportunities come to you." But from Mason's very down-to-earth viewpoint, this type of thinking was utter nonsense. Quitting a job without a suitable replacement was out of the question.

After eliminating some negative emotions about his present position, and then limiting decisions and beliefs about his abilities and options, Mason's thinking began to experience less turmoil and confusion. He came to realize that he hated injustice more than law and got passionate about other options which, previously, had not been available for contemplation.

The big breakthrough came when Mason started to think seriously about future goals. He discovered that he could start a blog where he could discuss pertinent issues, and decided to specialize in career counseling. Mason also realized that he could become a corporate trainer in six weeks, and instead of actively pursuing at law career, he could teach ad work with groups. He now has an exciting and very fulfilling career.

4. Be Realistic and Responsible or Go for It

With that in mind, the next conditions needed for a well formed goal are "Realistic" and "Responsible." The "Realistic" part of goal setting can be a bit tricky. On the one hand, one hears, "Do not underestimate yourself; the sky is the limit!" and on the other, "You have to be realistic." Does one take the plunge or hang onto one's day job? If we have never done something before, how can we realistically assume it will come to pass?

Instructions to the Reader

A good suggestion is to look around and notice if what you want has been achieved by other people in similar situations as yours. If the answer is yes, then probably this could be realistic. However, you alone are the judge here, and it is solely your decision. If your past experiences in accomplishing your goals have been extremely positive, make your goal more ambitious. In a reversed situation, if you did not get many of your previous goals, make your goal less impressive and more down-to-earth.

Whenever you set a goal, consider the consequences of setting it. Look at these three levels to verify whether your goal is in correct alignment with your environment. You can ask yourself the following questions: "How will this goal change or affect me? How will this goal affect or change the people around me?" Here you can include your immediate family, close associates, friends, people at your work place, or in other circles you may belong to, as well as your community at large. When you do this part of the process, you have attended to the "Responsible" part of the goal.

5. Timed and Toward what you want

Finally, if all the steps described so far have been fulfilled, by now one should have a clear idea of the time frame necessary for the accomplishment of one's goal as well as the positive wording and mental imagery associated with it.

By following this process, although there are no guarantees of success in life, we can make sure that we are "arranging" for success. As for the reward that comes from taking risks, if we have always achieved our goals, then we have not aimed high enough to discover our full potential.

When we spend some time to think through these principles for a well-formed outcome or goal, paradoxically, we also create a path which leads to its fulfillment. This is not just a plan; it is a test set up by us and for us. If the answers do not add up, we need to alter our goal to make it more realistic. We might even decide to change to a different goal, or improve the first description to suit our new discoveries.

Overall, it is a good idea to have goals in different areas of life, in order to create balance. We all have friends or coworkers who are so taken by their career goals that they have little time left for anything else. Therefore, a good suggestion is to have balanced goals. If we think about different contexts of life as a wheel or a pizza pie, imagine each piece representing an area of life. If a piece is missing, the "wheel" will bounce along making for a rough ride.

When a part of our life lacks attention, even if other areas are richly rewarded, an aspect of our development is missing. To improve our overall level of satisfaction, we must create goals in the six key areas of life: career, family, relationships, health and fitness, spirituality, and personal growth, and development.

The reader should feel free to modify this list, as there are many variations on these grand themes of life, and only the reader can decide what constitutes a balanced life for him/herself.

A Time Line Goals Experience

Before we build additional skills, let us link what we have discussed so far to the future event time line process described in the chapter "A Time Line Experiment."

After one has completed the SMART process from the previous section, one can use the following steps to plant the seed of a future goal in one's future time line.

1. Know the last step.

Instructions to the Reader

Knowing the last step that has to happen so that you know you have achieved your goal is a key element that makes a difference between goals that have an excellent chance of success, and those that are more a matter of chance. Overall, if you really target a specific goal, it means that you have a clear and precise idea of what you want. You want X, and not "whatever happens to be." Therefore, to leave it to chance would be like you already give up on having what you want.

The question to ask yourself is, "What is the last thing that must happen for me to know that I have achieved my goal?"

The aim is to be able to say, "Yes – X' happened, and so I know that I have achieved my goal."

Will you know because of a statement from your bank account? Will it be because you signed a contract for your new job? Will it be because you have a date with the person of your dreams? It can be a symbolic moment, such as having a housewarming party for your new home, or the first day in a new career. Maybe it is the moment when you get the date with the person of your dream?

As you consider the last step, make sure you envisage it as a picture. It could be a still picture or a movie.

2. Turn the last step into an image.

Instructions to the Reader

Ideally, the last step will be a combination of a visual picture, with positive and pleasant sounds, happy or overall positive feelings, and if appropriate even tastes and smells. You could also add a healthy dose of empowering self-talk to the picture. You could say to yourself a few good words like: "Yes, I did it!" make note of this picture as you will use it in your time line.

3. Step into the image, looking through your own eyes.

After discovering the image of the last thing that has to happen so that one knows one has achieved one's goal, the next step is to make sure one is looking at everything through one's own eyes in that picture.

Instructions to the Reader

This means that (1) you do not see yourself in the picture and (2) that you are, in fact, part of that picture. It is critical at this point that you experience positive feelings, like the joy of accomplishing what you want.

NOTE TO THE READER: AS PREVIOUSLY DISCUSSED, THE UNCONSCIOUS MIND IS THE PART OF US THAT OPERATES EMOTIONALLY AND SYMBOLICALLY. THIS PICTURE IS A SYMBOL OF THE GOAL. IF YOU HAVE NO FEELINGS IN YOUR PICTURE, YOU DO NOT INVOLVE YOUR UNCONSCIOUS MIND

AT THE LEVEL IT SHOULD BE INVOLVED, AND THIS MAY
HAVE UNDESIRABLE CONSEQUENCES IN THAT,
UNCONSCIOUSLY, YOU MAY NOT HAVE ENOUGH
MOTIVATION TO PURSUE THAT GOAL.

4. Adjust the qualities to make this image as desirable as possible.

At the end of this process, one should experience a very motivating and positive feeling about one's picture of the final thing that must happen to know that one got his/her goal or outcome. If one does not, something went amiss. Then, one should review the previous instructions and repeat the process.

Instructions to the Reader

Now that you have the picture of the last step, and you are looking through your own eyes feeling the feelings of joy and accomplishment, at this point, you will adjust the qualities of this picture to create the greatest positive feeling of desire for it. The easiest way of thinking of this process is to think of your computer screen. Imagine that the picture you are working with is contained on a screen in your mind and imagine that you have a personal photoshop available to make adjustments to qualities of that image. You can adjust the brightness, the color, the focus, the size of the picture, the sound, and the feelings themselves. If your inner picture is in black and white, change it to color, and notice if it gives you a better feeling of desire for it. If not, leave it exactly as it was before. If it is in color, turn up the colors and make them more rich and saturated. Does that increase the intensity of the positive feelings of desire for your goal? If yes, leave it like that. If not, try turning down the intensity of the color so that it becomes more pastel.

Next is the brightness. Take the brightness level and turn it up. Make it brighter and brighter, but not so bright that it washes out. Notice the result. Does the picture appear even more pleasing now? If it does not increase the positive feeling, turn down the brightness so that it is like in an intimate scene. Notice what gives you the most intense, positive feeling and leave the picture with these qualities.

After that, follow the same process for the focus. Make the focus crisp, sharp, and clear. If this move increases the positive feeling leave it like that, and if it does not, try defocusing it slightly. Notice which one gives you the most positive feeling and allow your image to stay like that.

Try turning the image into a movie if it is a still frame, or vice-versa, and notice which one pleases you the most.

Still looking through your own eyes, try to move the whole picture closer to you and notice if that increases the level of positive feelings. If it does, bring it closer until the feeling is at a maximum level. If not, move the picture a little further away and notice if that move increases the positive feelings. Leave the picture in the best location and distance so that it has the maximum positive feeling for you.

Now adjust all the sounds. Are there any sounds in your image? If sounds are not present, then maybe you should add some sounds that please you. If no sounds are necessary, then move on to the next step. But if sounds are already present, turn up the volume and notice if the whole image is improved. Sometimes people have more positive feelings by turning down the volume. Try that and see which one gives you the most positive feelings.

If other people are present, notice what they are saying to you.

Observe what you are saying to yourself. Change the volume up or down, and see which one increases the positive feelings.

After the sounds, pay attention to the feelings. Become aware of what you are feeling and notice that you can actually turn up the intensity of those feelings. Most people have at least a feeling of happiness, satisfaction, or fulfillment. How could it not feel good to have created what you want?

When you are done, make sure the picture has the most positive feeling it can possibly have. Simply put, make sure that your desire for this goal has been maximized.

5. Step out of the image so you see your body in the picture.

Now, the next step is again a critical step in making the difference between achievable and less achievable goals.

Instructions to the Reader

Once you have adjusted the qualities of the inner image of the last step, leave your body in the picture, and in your mind, step out so that you observe the picture from an external viewpoint. Make sure you see yourself in the image, enjoying the successful achievement of that goal. If you do not see your body in the picture, you literally cut yourself out of it. This may seem like a trivial detail, but it is extremely important, as we previously saw in the section "A Taste of transformation."

6. Float above the time line

Instructions to the Reader

Next imagine you take that picture in your hands, as you float above your time line, and then float over the future to the designated time. This is the time you have decided for the accomplishment of the goal.

7. Drop the picture in the time line

Instruction to the Reader

Insert the image into your time line at the correct point. As you do, follow it along and notice how it goes down into your time line at the precise moment.

8. Float back to the now-moment.

Instructions to the Reader

Float back above the time line to the now-moment, and become aware of your present location. Come back into the now, into the room, and observe your surroundings to "ground" yourself.

Using Temporal Language

It is interesting to watch somebody arrange flowers into a beautiful bouquet. While watching, it becomes quickly apparent that the flowers become a different visual experience with a different arrangement. Sometimes even with just a few quick adjustments from a person who has a knack for it. Words related to time are very much like a bunch of flowers that need a skillful hand. Here, we show the reader how to arrange words so that they create a different experience of time in the mind.

As the reader will recall, we learned to state things in the positive, because this gives strong direction to our unconscious minds. Using temporal, that is to say, time-related language, helps us to conceive of events in the appropriate area of our time line. This is a great practice if one is also attempting to change the shape, or the orientation of the time line.

Temporal language can help one talk to him/herself more effectively, but it is well-known for being more effective if used with other people. The best place to start is with the basic idea of putting all problems where they belong – in the past. Let us investigate a simple example. "The problem *I had* with the fear of elevators, is *now gone*."

Notice the words "*had*" and "*now gone*." The implication is that the old problem is really not in the present anymore, but somewhere in the past. Compare this with the popular belief that worries, anxieties, and even phobias repeat themselves forever. Notice the word "*forever*." The implication here is that there will never be a time when that problem is gone.

It may sound funny or untrue to speak about problems in the past tense, rather than saying, "I am experiencing anxiety in elevators," but we suggest that when one does it this way, it gives the unconscious mind a different milestone.

Similarly, if a manager has a problem with the sales team, it would be advisable to refer to the problem as though it were in the past rather than dragging it through the present and into the future. For instance, the manager could say, "We did not do very well last week, but that was last week. We have changed some things, and at the end of this week, we will say, "this was a great week."

Instructions to the Reader

Follow along with this statement and try to unpack it in your mind. Particularly, notice what pictures are formed as you utter the words slowly. Also, note that your mind's imagery is left on a positive picture which, just by itself, and if the unconscious mind accepts it as a suggestion for the future, may contribute to a change in behavior. Correspondingly, notice that the feelings change as the words flow through the sentence. If nothing else, it is unquestionably more uplifting for the team.

Using the past tense for future goals, puts more emphasis on the solution and brings it to the foreground in the present. This resourceful language also highlights any internal resistance you have to the problem being in the past. Sometimes we hang onto our problems out of comfort and familiarity, so speaking about them in the past tense will put the problems where they belong – in the past.

This is the reason why we encourage you to use a carefully crafted language when you sent goals for the future. Here is the formula:

"IT IS NOW (HERE, INSERT THE FUTURE DATE FOR YOUR GOAL), AND OUR STARTUP IS PROFITABLE AS WE CONTINUE THE PRESENT SALES TREND. OUR STAFF IS ENTIRELY MOTIVATED AND PERFORMING WELL."

Note the word "is." This presupposes reality rather than potentiality. We carefully avoided "will be," "should be," "can be," "may be," or the dreaded future tense forms, such as "profitability will be expected to occur in two months."

After all, thinking of future goals as being in the "here and now" means you have no concealed or hidden worries that may creep in next November. It also means that it is time to act, rather than putting things off.

Jordan's Experience With His Time Line

Jordan is an old acquaintance who does not do the same type of work as we do. She is a scientist, and her opinion is that soft sciences are too flaky. Her world is full of precise reasoning with meticulous rules. In this world, there is only black or white—no shades of gray. She initially ignored the good use of Time Line Therapy® techniques, thinking them too speculative, but she agreed to "play" with finding her time line. As it was to be expected, her time line stretched in front of her from right to left, with the future to the left and the past to the right.

One day, another car rear-ended her vehicle. Although the accident was not serious, she was furious and frustrated. When we met again, to our amazement, she told us that there was no future in her time line. She had a past, and she could easily imagine it on the time line, but there was no perceptible future. She could not imagine any future. In her time line, the past, was like looking down a freeway or at a "ribbon" of time, but the future just was not there anymore.

With a few specific questions and a little research on our part, she realized that her past and future were both clustered together like a tangled mass of rubber behind her, and her present was a short stub, charred and sticking out of her back. Needless to say, this was probably not a useful time line.

Apparently, she was so preoccupied with dealing with the

---

effects of the accident, and the repairs to her car, that unconsciously, she had formed her past and future into a glob that obstructed her view of all other possibilities. Together, we spent some time "untangling the glob," by letting go of negative emotions from the accident, and after that, we let go of the beliefs and decisions she had made about the future and the past.

At the end of this process, her time line stretched itself out again, all of its own accord. She could see her future again, only this time, the present was right where she was, the past was behind her, and the future was in front.

It is significant to notice that her time line was scrambled when she had a cluster of negative emotions tangled together in that event and that her time line changed all by itself after she let the negative emotions go.

For the moment, she decided to let the orientation of her time line be from front to back, in an In-Time organization, but after a couple of weeks, she changed it back like it was in the old days. This process opened her up to the future, and to having a different experience of life. On the weekends, she gives herself an In-Time time line, to experience time with less stress and more relaxation.

Focus, Desire, and Action

The average person is guided unconsciously by his or her emotions. S/he is likely to think that everyone else is doing the same. Positive emotions, if used correctly, can be great incentives for actions and motivation. Not only do we act according to our feelings, but in most cases we also think according to them. Instead of finding the real reasons for our actions and behaviors we usually find excuses to justify our actions, which are in accordance with our feelings. Most of our reasoning is done to justify our feelings or to find proof for the position dictated by our desires, feelings, or our agreements.

Unfortunately, our emotions also dictate our focus. We focus on what makes us not feel bad, instead of focusing on what could make us feel good, and yes, there is a difference. As a result, we repeatedly keep creating situations and circumstances that reflect back to us what we are focusing on.

Most people are not trained to understand that thoughts and ideas are widely determined by our interests. When we begin to analyze our interests, we find that they are largely a result of our feelings and emotions. We like certain things, and our interests follow our likes. Not only do feelings determine what we think about but also how we think about it. In other words, our judgments are influenced by, and shaped in direct relation to, how we are feeling even if those feelings are unconscious. It is much easier to approve of the actions of someone we like or whose views are similar to ours than of someone's whose personality and opinions we do not support. It is also appropriate, although not well-known, to acknowledge that we tend to find what we look for in things and people. And this is all inter-related with our feelings.

When we take a closer look at our thinking and behavior, we find that it is almost entirely dependent on the state of desire for its motivation. The mind will operate in alignment with the strongest desire of the moment. Therefore, someone whose desires are not well-defined or someone who has no desires will find that their mind wanders continuously. In the end, our behavior will depend a lot on our focus.

So far our discussion has focused on the negative aspects of our emotions. Feelings and emotions are generally inner states and the difference between them and desire is that desire seeks to transform itself into behavior. Desire is the great motivator in life, and it provides a great incentive to take action. A person's life and achievements largely reflect the quality and degree of this person's desires. No matter how intelligent an individual is, and no matter how great his/her powers of reasoning, judgment, and discrimination are, unless s/he also possesses a strong desire for accomplishment, s/he will not achieve very much.

Not only are achievements and attainments determined by our desires, but overall, our life largely depends on our desires. They are also responsible for which road we travel upon, and for how far we travel on that road. Many people do not manifest many of their secret desires. Mentally, they find reasons to excuse themselves, often saying that motivation is simply lacking

But it is not a well-known fact that, often desires end in wanting, and that wanting never reaches a stage of action. A desire left unexpressed is like a car that hasn't been started. Start the car and put the foot on the accelerator and the car begins to move. In all walks of life people who have achieved many accomplishments have had an incredibly strong desire for attainment, achievement, and an overall happy and fulfilling life.

Willpower is not what one needs, but desire. Desire takes the energy of emotion and moves it into behavior. No matter how clearly a person may see what s/he wants in the future, no matter how perfectly s/he envisions the plan of action, unless s/he has the desire to do something about it, there will be no action.

Desire can be cultivated, like a rose grown in a garden. The reader will be well advised to remember that mastery comes as the basic and intermediate abilities, desires, and actions become habitual, that is to say, that they become unconscious, like reflexes. This explains much of the mystery and efficiency used by masterful people in any area of endeavor, especially the "mysteries" regarding change and personal excellence. The human mind remains the most beautiful, amazing, awe-inspiring, and enigmatic frontier.

Made in the USA
Henderson, Nevada
September, 2016